A companionable and [...]
writings. Helpful, us[...]

The [...]   s

This is a fantastic resource, full of insights and wide-ranging applications of the life and legacy of the beloved C. S. Lewis. Whether in the classroom, a church, or a small group study, *Walking With C. S. Lewis* will help readers go deeper not only in their knowledge and appreciation of Lewis, but in their own spiritual journey. Far more than just a teaching curriculum, this is resource for cultivating virtue and inspiring curiosity, beckoning us (as Lewis might say) to "Come further up, come further in!"

—BRETT McCRACKEN, journalist and author of *Uncomfortable: The Awkward and Essential Challenge of Christian Community* and *Hipster Christianity: When Church and Cool Collide*

Walking with C. S. Lewis combines important summary discussions of the books covered in the series with probing, exploratory questions. Who was C. S. Lewis? What were his important books? Why are his books still popular more than 50 years after his death? What does Lewis have to say to us today? These and many other questions are considered in *Walking with C. S. Lewis*. Book clubs, church groups, and Sunday school classes will find a wealth of material in these two helpful resources.

—DON W. KING, professor of English, Montreat College; author of *C. S. Lewis, Poet* and *The Collected Poems of C. S. Lewis: A Critical Edition*

WALKING WITH C. S. LEWIS

A COMPANION GUIDE

WALKING WITH C. S. LEWIS

A Spiritual Journey Through His Life and Writings

A COMPANION GUIDE

RYAN J. PEMBERTON

LEXHAM PRESS

Print ISBN 9781577997696
Digital ISBN 9781577997702

Lexham Editorial: Abigail Stocker, Joel Wilcox
Cover Design: Bryan Hintz
Back Cover Design: [TBD]
Typesetting: ProjectLuz.com

CONTENTS

INTRODUCTION

WELCOME TO *WALKING WITH C. S. LEWIS*! IN THIS STUDY, WE will be digging into some of the most well-known books from renowned author and Christian apologist C. S. Lewis. While Lewis's work might appear to be the subject of our time together, the goal of this project is not to grow closer to Lewis's work, but to grow closer to God. Lewis's writings have helped people all over the world better understand the Christian faith and the Lord of all creation in meaningful, life-changing ways. In this series, we will use Lewis's writing as a lens that clarifies our view of Jesus Christ and his redemptive work in this world, so that we might better live into the Christian faith.

If you're using this study companion in conjunction with the *Walking with C. S. Lewis* video series, you'll also gain Professor Tony Ash's summary of Lewis's works and their personal impact on him. Filmed in a number of historic locations in and around Oxford, England—where Lewis spent much of his life—Professor Ash will guide us through each work, pointing out themes and ideas to pay special attention to. This study guide will help you discover even more about each work.

HOW TO USE THIS STUDY GUIDE

ALONGSIDE THE VIDEOS

This study guide is designed to complement the *Walking with C. S. Lewis* video series, featuring Professor Tony Ash. This work will provide a broader background for each of the C. S. Lewis works discussed in this video series, go deeper into those themes and topics that Professor Ash introduces but doesn't have time to discuss further, and ask thought-provoking questions to help guide your own studies. By using this study guide hand-in-hand with the *Walking with C. S. Lewis* videos, you will take even more away from C. S. Lewis's rich writing and from the video series.

SECTION-BY-SECTION REFLECTION

Most episodes of this study are broken up into several sections. This guide will provide a brief summary of what has been discussed in each episode of the video series; an explanation of points or ideas that Professor Ash introduced but wasn't able to flesh out further; and suggest several questions that you may find helpful for reflection.

You will also find background information on the C. S. Lewis books being studied, quotes, and little-known facts about

C. S. Lewis sprinkled throughout each chapter in this guide. These perks are designed to enrich your experience with Lewis's sometimes-dense writing.

After watching the entire video series, you can also return to this guide and see how the questions and takeaways provided here can help guide your reflections on Professor Ash's teaching about Lewis's work.

FAITH-BUILDING MATERIALS FOR LIFE

Throughout this series, remember: the purpose of this study is not merely for you to know more about C. S. Lewis the Christian, the apologist, or the writer. The goal of *Walking with C. S. Lewis* is that, through Lewis's work, you better understand and grow into the Christian life. Think of these as faith-building materials for the Christian journey with C. S. Lewis as our guide, and with Professor Tony Ash as our guide to C. S. Lewis.

EPISODE ONE

MERE CHRISTIANITY

DID YOU KNOW?

C. S. Lewis's radio broadcast talks were delivered throughout the whole of England via BBC radio during World War II. Lewis's broadcast talks were so popular that he became the most recognized voice in England after Winston Churchill.

Christianity Today named *Mere Christianity* book of the century in the magazine's April 2000 issue. More than 100 of the magazine's contributors and church leaders were asked to nominate the top-ten religious books of the past century. C. S. Lewis was far and away the top author, and his *Mere Christianity* was the most frequently chosen book.

Of all the broadcast talks Lewis recorded for BBC radio, only one survives to this day: "The New Men." Apart from this sole recording from his broadcast talks, listeners can find other audio recordings of Lewis in "The C. S. Lewis Recordings," which includes a talk on his book *The Four Loves*, his introduction to *The Great Divorce*, and other talks. After imagining Lewis's words from his books, readers will appreciate hearing his booming accent for themselves.

C. S. Lewis was asked to give a series of talks on the Christian faith to the entire BBC listening audience just 10 years after his own conversion to Christianity.

C. S. Lewis's radio broadcast talks were not pre-recorded, but delivered live from the BBC's London radio station. Lewis would commute from his home in Oxford to London to deliver the talk, and then return late the same night (roughly a one-hour trip each way).

Lewis's broadcast talks were incredibly popular, earning Lewis a large following and an almost equally large pile of letters. Not all of his listeners were warm to Lewis's talks, however. In fact, Lewis heard from the BBC with a report of listener research, informing him of the split response, between those who regarding him as either "the cat's whiskers" or "beneath contempt." Lewis rightly dismissed this response, assuring the BBC the response actually had little to do with him (see his letter to Eric Fenn at the BBC, dated 25 March 1944).

FROM ATHEIST TO WORLD-FAMOUS CHRISTIAN APOLOGIST

For our first video in *Walking with C. S. Lewis*, we will be looking at one of Lewis's most well-known books: *Mere Christianity*. But before Professor Ash digs into this modern classic, he offers some background on Lewis's influence in his life (intro video), followed by some background on the surprising early life of the Christian author C. S. Lewis. We will spend much more time looking at Lewis's life and the experience that shaped his work later in this series (Episode 4), but it's worthwhile to begin our study with some context.

Though he is known today as one of the greatest Christian writers of the past century, it is still surprising to some that Lewis spent many of his adult years as an atheist. Indeed, it is because Lewis personally wrestled with doubt and critiques of Christianity for years before becoming Christian himself that he is so appealing to many readers today.

As Professor Ash notes, Lewis didn't wait to begin his writing career until after his Christian conversion—even when he was young, it always seemed that Lewis was writing something. As a young boy, Lewis loved to write imaginative stories of animals dressed in human clothes and involved in chivalrous adventures—a sign of things to come! Later, as a teenager and a young adult, Lewis dreamed of literary success in poetry. And yet it wasn't until *after* his Christian conversion that Lewis began to find any real success in his writing.

As a young atheist, C. S. Lewis published two separate books of poetry, neither of which achieved the literary success Lewis dreamed of. But it was after C. S. Lewis came to the Christian faith in his early thirties that he began to receive widespread praise for his writing. In Lewis's first book published after his Christian conversion, *The Pilgrim's Regress*—a play on John Bunyan's classic allegory, *The Pilgrim's Progress*, and a retelling of Lewis's own faith journey—we see hints of the highly imaginative and deeply logical writing that would lead to Lewis's worldwide fame as a Christian apologist and writer.

FOR REFLECTION

1 Professor Ash notes several reasons for Lewis's widespread success to this day, including the fact that though he was clearly brilliant, Lewis managed to write for the "common man." We have also talked here about several other reasons for the popularity of Lewis's work. For those of us familiar with Lewis's writings, why did you first connect with his books? What does that tell us about how we might bring the beauty of the Christian message to others using our own God-given gifts?

2 In this first section, C. S. Lewis is described as an "evange-list," even though, as Professor Ash notes, Lewis didn't call himself an evangelist. Why does Professor Ash describe Lewis in this way? Does this change how you think about the word "evangelist"?

FIRST MEETING
C. S. LEWIS'S WORK

A FTER INTRODUCING US TO A BIT OF C. S. LEWIS'S STORY, Professor Ash shares how he first encountered Lewis's work while looking for cheap books as a college student. The first C. S. Lewis book that Professor Ash ever read was the very same book we'll be focusing on in this chapter: *Mere Christianity*. Not expecting anything so widely recommended and praised to be thoughtful or rich enough to be worth reading, Professor Ash shares his surprise at the depth of thought and precision he found in Lewis's writing:

> I was amazed by the clarity with which it was written. I was amazed by the illustrative power of the author. I was amazed at how difficult concepts were made clear and plain, and how there was a depth to the discussion of the issues that were discussed in this book that I had never seen before ... I had never had my soul stirred the way it was stirred by reading *Mere Christianity* and by what C. S. Lewis had to say.

Professor Ash's life—like so many others'—turned a corner after reading C. S. Lewis. Though he was already a Christian, his faith took on another level of richness and depth after this book. As he puts it, "I was ushered into a new experience in my Christian life that gave me a larger picture than I'd ever had before."

During a time in which Professor Ash was studying theology and encountering ideas that troubled his religious views, Lewis's writing helped support and even grow Professor Ash's Christian faith. As he puts it, reading Lewis "gave [him] an anchor." This early experience launched Professor Ash on a career of reading and teaching C. S. Lewis's books that would span several decades.

FOR REFLECTION

1 Professor Ash shares how he would quote C. S. Lewis in his sermons so frequently that people would notice if he *didn't* quote Lewis. Do you have a favorite C. S. Lewis quotation? How has it been helpful in your own faith? Have you been able to share it with others?

2 As he puts it, reading *Mere Christianity* supported and expanded Professor Ash's Christian faith. Did you have a similar first encounter with C. S. Lewis? Or, did you come to Christianity after reading Lewis's writing? What about Lewis's books speaks to you most?

WORLD WAR II AND THE BBC
RADIO BROADCAST TALKS

A T THE END OF THE LAST SECTION, PROFESSOR ASH HINTED AT the origins of *Mere Christianity*. It is surprising for some to hear that this modern classic did not actually begin as a book, but as a series of broadcast talks on BBC radio. Thanks to Lewis's thoughtful take on *The Problem of Pain* (which we'll look at more in Episode 3), the BBC invited C. S. Lewis—who was then working full-time as an Oxford don, tutoring students and delivering lectures—to record a series of talks on the topic of "The Christian Faith as a I See It—by a Layman." Commuting by train from his home in Oxford to London each week to record these live radio broadcasts, Lewis wrote these talks during the heat of World War II, which clearly shaped his message.

The early 1940s were an extremely busy time for Lewis. In addition to teaching, he was also writing, delivering lectures to members of the Royal Air Force, and preaching. It was during this time that Lewis delivered a famous lecture called "Learning in Wartime," which concerned the question of whether it was irresponsible to be studying during a global war. England itself was under the threat of air raids—London children were sent to the country in hopes that their lives might be spared—and food was being drastically rationed. But in the historic city of Oxford, England, students and faculty continued their studies. *How does this wartime period change the human situation?* Lewis's lecture asked. His response? It doesn't; it just makes us more aware of our continual situation as humans.

Christians always face the reality of their own mortality, Lewis notes, whether war is taking place or not. And because of this, questions of life and death are constantly before us. But the war had an undeniable impact on Lewis's audience and the popularity of his radio broadcasts. With his listeners facing the very real threat of their own deaths at any moment, Lewis's broadcasts found a captivated audience that was hungry to know what Christianity had to say to their own situation, and he communicated it powerfully and clearly. Indeed, it was during these radio broadcast talks that C. S. Lewis's voice became the most recognized voice in all of England after Winston Churchill, then the prime minister of the United Kingdom.

FOR REFLECTION

1   At the time Lewis delivered these BBC radio broadcast talks, much of England had already moved away from its Christian roots. But Lewis's presentation of Christian ideas came at an important time—during World War II. How would the timing of Lewis's broadcast talks have changed the way its first audience would have received it? How do your own circumstances change your reading of *Mere Christianity*?

2 Find and read Lewis's lecture "Learning in Wartime." (It isn't very long!) Do you agree with Lewis that war does not change our human condition, but merely emphasizes the reality of death? How does your view of this reality change how you speak about Christianity with non-Christians?

READING *MERE CHRISTIANITY*

A S PROFESSOR ASH NOTES, C. S. LEWIS DELIVERED THESE BBC radio broadcast talks just 10 years after his Christian conversion. Neither is Lewis a trained theologian. And yet, here he is dealing with some of the most complex, important issues of the Christian faith—and he could not seem more experienced or comfortable. But far from being a drawback, the fact that C. S. Lewis was not a theologian or a minister but simply a lay Christian was precisely *why* he was first asked to speak about the Christian faith on air to the nation's listeners. It was also for these two reasons that his Oxford colleagues largely regarded Lewis's broadcast talks with contempt.

While *Mere Christianity* covers an incredible number of Christian teachings, Professor Ash focuses on just two: Christian unity and character.

UNITY

First, Professor Ash notes that while Lewis's writing may not have all the answers for how to see true Christian unity in our world,

Lewis's concern with the topic is a great beginning; recognizing the church's fractures as a problem is an important first step toward a solution.

The importance of this topic isn't simply a personal cause of concern for Lewis; it's built on Jesus' own heart for his followers. As Professor Ash highlights, during the very end of his earthly ministry, Jesus prays to God the Father for unity among his followers: "That they may all be one, just as you, Father, are in me, and I in you" (John 17:21). The Apostle Paul echoes this same idea when he writes that the Church is not a dismembered body, but a unified body: "So we, though many, are one body in Christ, and individually members one of another" (Rom 12:5; see also 1 Cor 12:5, 27). Lewis is right to underline the importance of corporate oneness for Christians.

But Lewis is not merely concerned with *articulating* the Christian vision of unity; he *models* Christian unity throughout his work, including here in *Mere Christianity*. How does he do that? By choosing not to focus on the doctrines or practices that divide Christians. Instead, he discusses those traditions that all Christians have in common—on "mere" Christianity, as it were. It is for that reason that *Mere Christianity*—and Lewis's writing in general—has had such universal appeal. Even those who don't share the particularities of Lewis's practice of Anglican Christian faith are deeply indebted to him for showing them what it means to be a follower of Jesus Christ. (Indeed, while I was a tour guide of C. S. Lewis's former home, The Kilns, as a scholar-in-residence during my days as an Oxford University student, I was taken aback by how many different countries were represented by guests who traveled hundreds, even thousands, of miles to see the home of this writer. It was not unusual for a week's guests to include visitors from Korea, Eastern Europe, North America, and South America.)

CHARACTER

Another key idea in *Mere Christianity* is that of character. Like Christian unity, discussion of character is often missing from current conversations—but Lewis saw it as incredibly important to the Christian life. Here, Lewis is concerned with emphasizing the fact that God wants people of a certain character, and it is that kind of character that is characteristic of heaven and the kingdom of God. While it would be wrong to completely remove practices from our conversation on character—as they work together, not apart—Professor Ash notes Lewis's emphasis that what Christ is interested in is people whose lives embody the character of heaven in the here and now. What this means is that Christians should not simply be interested in doing the right things, but doing the right things for the right reason. For even the right actions can be done for the wrong reasons.

To help make this point, Lewis uses an analogy of how a well-trained tennis player would differ from an amateur (Chapter 2, Book 3, *Mere Christianity*). Now, the amateur tennis player may get a good shot in here and there, but it may be due more to luck than anything else. The tennis player who is well trained, by contrast, has formed a certain character of shot that is more likely to produce the right shot, at the right time, for the right reason. This analogy can be a helpful way to think of the importance of Christian character. For the Christian is to be formed in the likeness of Jesus Christ. As Lewis puts it in elsewhere in *Mere Christianity*, the whole point of Christianity is that we would become "little Christs."

I was once giving a tour of the Kilns to a woman who said her problem with Christianity is that it has so many rules. But that is a misconception of what Christianity is: rather than as a set of rules, Christianity is better understood as a way of being in the world. It is an embodiment of God's heavenly kingdom in our present reality, which longs for Jesus' return. This embodiment of God's kingdom was perfectly instantiated in the person of Jesus Christ. And, after his life, death, and resurrection, he has invited us to embody this same reality, empowered by the Holy Spirit. This is far different than understanding Christianity as a long list of permissions and prohibitions. As Lewis notes: "We might think that God wanted simply obedience to a set of rules: whereas He really wants people of a particular sort" (Chapter 2, Book 3, *Mere Christianity*).

OTHER IDEAS IN *MERE CHRISTIANITY*

Professor Ash introduces a list of other key ideas in *Mere Christianity* that he does not have time to go into further, but which are hugely important for Christians to consider. These include the relationship between the physical and spiritual life; what Jesus meant when he said, "Be ye perfect"; the sin of pride; why all Christians aren't "nicer" than non-Christians; forgiveness; Christian marriage; and why Jesus was not simply a great moral teacher. While all of these topics are worthwhile to consider, we'll consider just three here.

NICE PEOPLE OR NEW MEN

First: at the start of the chapter "Nice People or New Men?" (Chapter 10, Book 4, *Mere Christianity*), C. S. Lewis introduces the often-asked question, "If Christianity is true why are not all Christians obviously nicer than non-Christians?"

In response to this common question, Lewis makes several points. First, he notes that while Christianity should, indeed, result in improvement in the individual who comes to Christian faith ("You will recognize them by their fruits," Matt 7:16), it does not make sense to compare someone who is a Christian to someone who is not a Christian and expect the comparison to be fair. The reason, as Lewis points out: if you are concerned with the difference the Christian faith makes on a life, then you must consider a particular life both before and after they have become a Christian.

For example, if someone who is not a Christian has a naturally calm, warm temperament, it does not make sense to compare them to someone else who has a naturally bitter personality, who is a Christian, and expect to have an argument against Christianity. Rather, as Lewis notes, you should ask what the person with a naturally calm temperament would be like if they became Christian—the impact this conversion would have on the rest of their life. Further, while acknowledging unfinished growth in the naturally bitter person, it's worth asking what they would be like if they *weren't* Christian. In examining the difference that Christ and Christianity make, the question must always be: what effect do they have on a particular life?

Second, Lewis looks at the word "nice." People often think that Christianity is interested in is making "nicer" people—but that isn't the case. As we've already noted, what Christ—and so, too, Christianity—is concerned with is making people of a particular quality, best described as characteristic of the kingdom of God here on earth. The goal of Christianity, as the Lord's Prayer teaches us, is that God's kingdom would come, and that it would begin right here in our lives, because of Christ's work on and in and through us. That work may very well result in "nicer" people, but we would be mistaken to think that's the primary concern of Christianity; there even may be situations in which being a Christian does not mean being "nicer."

As Lewis notes, what this question suggests is that there are certain people who are not naturally nice who need the help Christianity offers, and that there are others—who *are* naturally nice—who do not need to bother with such things. But that mistake has infinite importance. A naturally warm disposition is not something the person in question is likely even responsible for; it is, instead, a gift from God. And so, to compliment them for it is, in a way, giving credit where credit is not due.

The end goal of Christianity is not to produce a nice person, but a new creation (see Chapter 10, Book 4, *Mere Christianity*).

THE GREAT SIN

Another important idea in *Mere Christianity* that Professor Ash touches on is that of the "Great Sin": pride. The third book of *Mere Christianity* concerns Christian behavior. And the issue of pride lies at the heart of this conversation. The reason, as Lewis notes, is because pride is at the root of all other vices; "it is the complete anti-God state of mind" (Chapter 8, Book 3, *Mere Christianity*). Pride is unique, compared to other vices, in that it is essentially competitive: pride always is invested in comparisons between others and myself. In the process, pride will lead me to put myself at odds with others. We see this at work in our lives in numerous ways. For example, it isn't enough for me to take pleasure in my child learning how to read; I must, instead, compare her reading performance to other children. Or, it isn't enough to celebrate the publication of my first book; I must compare it to other books' success or failure. In this way, pride turns people who are supposed to be our neighbors—enjoyed in a relationship of love and care— into enemies with whom we only compete.

Ultimately, Lewis suggests, the competitive nature of pride leads us into unhealthy relationships not only with other people, but also with God. We won't ever be able to compete with the God of all creation. But, more importantly, pride keeps us from knowing God: "Unless you know God as that [immeasurably superior to yourself]—and, therefore, know yourself as nothing in comparison—you do not know God at all" (Chapter 8, Book 3, *Mere Christianity*).

What, then, does Lewis offer as the solution for the Great Sin? His first suggestion: acknowledge your pride. As soon as he suggests this, we run into the problem of thinking that this point no longer applies to us, because we don't think highly of ourselves at all—but that would be a mistake. The opposite of pride is not thinking badly of yourself; even self-deprecation can be a form of pride when it causes your focus to remain on yourself ("You think that's bad? You'll never believe what I did!" someone might say). Lewis puts it this way: "Do not imagine that if you meet a really humble man he will be ... a sort of greasy, smarmy person, who is always telling you that, of course, he is nobody. Probably all you will think about him is that he seemed a cheerful, intelligent chap who took a real interest in what *you* said to him." After acknowledging our issue with pride, we must turn our gaze away from ourselves and toward God. This is, of course, not something we can do on our own; we must ask for God's help. And as our gaze moves from ourselves to God, embodied in the person of Jesus Christ, we will notice that God enables us to see others, for the first time, in love and not in competition.

A MORAL TEACHER

The last point we'll consider from *Mere Christianity* is one of my all-time personal favorites. When I first read it, it was one of the only times in my life when I have been forced to put down my book and think very seriously about what I had just read. Indeed, it led me to put both feet into Christianity for the first time in my life.

The point in question comes at the end of Chapter 3 of Book 2 of *Mere Christianity*, "The Shocking Alternative," in the form of a comment you may have heard someone say at one point or another: "I'm ready to accept Jesus as a great moral teacher, but I don't accept His claim to be God." Lewis's threefold response has come to be referred to as the "Trilemma"; "Mad, Bad, or God argument"; or the "Liar, Lunatic, or Lord argument." It goes like this: If Jesus said the kinds of things the Bible claims he said, then we only have three options. First, we can assume he is simply out of his mind, deranged, just as crazy as a man who tells others that he's a fried egg (and genuinely believes it!). Or, we can say he is a kind of person the world has never known, a megalomaniac who would make Hitler seem incredibly humble. Or, third and lastly, we can take him at his word: we can believe that he is, in fact, the creator of all that is, who entered into his own creation for the purpose of redeeming it and bringing it back to himself. His own claims about his identity don't leave us the option of calling him merely a great moral teacher.

The reason this passage so struck me when I first read it as a 19-year-old college student was because it was the first time I was brought to the point of having to reckon fully with the divinity of Jesus. Even though I had been attending and even involved in various Christian ministries for some time, and even though I believed the Christian story was the most beautiful story I had ever known, I had not yet wholly consented to the fact that Jesus was God. But when I put down my copy of *Mere Christianity* after first reading this passage all those years ago, that's what I realized I had to do. I did not believe Jesus was out of his mind—he actually made a lot of sense, and others in the Gospels seemed to agree. I didn't think he was prideful—which is only a glimmer of what he would be if he said the kind of things he is on record of saying in the Gospels—and I couldn't remember anyone critiquing Jesus for being prideful. On the contrary, even those who don't consider themselves Christian would likely say Jesus was humble—and this is precisely Lewis's point. My only remaining option was that Jesus was precisely who he and the Bible said he is: the Lord of all creation, in the flesh.

And if that's true, then Jesus changes everything. We can no longer take or leave his teaching, if he is God in the flesh; we must take his life as much as his words as the single most important source of authority and life for our own lives. "You must make your choice," Lewis writes. "You can shut Him up for a fool, you can spit at Him and kill Him as a demon; or you can fall at His feet and call Him Lord and God." And that's exactly what I did; it changed the rest of my life. It changed Professor Ash's life, too. Indeed, believing and living into this news has changed the lives of some of the most impactful women and men in the world. And it can change yours, too.

FOR REFLECTION

1 Professor Ash shares one of C. S. Lewis's well-known analogies—the image of Christianity as a great hallway, with many doors that lead to different rooms—to emphasize the importance of Christian unity. These rooms are distinct, but they are all connected by way of the central hallway. How does this analogy change or reflect the way *you* think about the global Christian church?

2 For some Christians, practice and beliefs are areas that feed disunity rather than unity. Christians who focus more on right ideas may focus less on the practices of the Christian faith; those in a tradition more concerned with right practices may think less about right ideas. In discussing Christian character, it is tempting to think that what we *do* doesn't matter as much as the type of people we *are*. How could this be misleading? How do our practices and our character work together?

3 According to Lewis, what are the problems with comparing Christians to non-Christians, particularly when asking who is "nicer"? Is being "nice" something that God cares about?

4 In his chapter on pride, Lewis suggests that those who are proud cannot know God. If this is true, why are Christians so often criticized for their pride? How can putting oneself down still be considered a form of pride?

5 Why would it be an issue to believe Jesus is merely a great teacher and not profess faith in him as God? Do you find Lewis's "Liar, Lunatic, or Lord" argument persuasive? What are some potential critiques of this argument?

EPISODE TWO

THE SCREWTAPE LETTERS

DID YOU KNOW?

C. S. Lewis's original title for this work was *As One Devil to Another*, which he suggested in a letter to his older brother, Warren.[1]

Lewis said that he decided to model the setting of hell on something like a modern bureaucracy, "in clean, carpeted, warmed and well-lighted offices, [inhabited] by quiet men with white collars" because this is where "the greatest evil" of our age is conceived (from the 1961 "new preface" to *The Screwtape Letters*).

IMAGINATIVE DEPICTIONS
OF JUDGMENT

IN THIS VIDEO, PROFESSOR ASH IS AT ST. JAMES THE GREAT church in South Leigh, England. As he points out, this location has a grand mural depicting the final judgment. On one side of this rendition of the event, the "accursed"—those who are condemned to eternal torment—are depicted by a group of people preparing to be devoured by a terrible creature. On the other side, the redeemed, or "blessed," are being accepted into God's presence. As Professor Ash notes, people's understanding of the final judgment and afterlife determines how they live, in many important ways.

Lewis takes up that point in *The Screwtape Letters*, his imaginary correspondence between an elder demon, Screwtape, and a young apprentice, Wormwood, whom he is training in the art of temptation. The object of this temptation is a human referred to throughout the book as Wormwood's "patient." Lewis wrote *The Screwtape Letters* from the perspective of hell, which readers would do well to keep in mind. If they do, they will be given a fresh look at the reality of temptation and the ways in which we are led to live in ways opposite to God's plan for us.

Another point that is important to keep in mind when reading *The Screwtape Letters*: Lewis did not think heaven and hell were two equal and opposite groups, competing for human souls. Such an understanding of good and evil is known as "dualism" and is not the view held by Christianity—even if many Christians hold this view. Lewis and orthodox Christianity alike both understand God to be wholly good (benevolent) and all powerful (omnipotent), and the devil and demons, by contrast, to be originally good but willfully fallen into evil. In contrast to dualism, Christianity teaches that there is no equal and opposing power to God: God rules over all and is bringing about his purposes, even in this period between the first coming of his Son and his Son's final return and redemption of creation, known as the final judgment.

FOR REFLECTION

1   There are many different understandings of what the end and eternity will be like. Even within Christianity, people hold different views of eternity. Some believe that those who are not with God in the resurrection will simply cease to exist (annihilationism); others believe that those in hell will be tormented for eternity and those in heaven will live in an eternal state of glory; and still others believe that all will, ultimately, be united with God through Christ (Universalism). Different Christians have understood the afterlife in very different ways. Why does Professor Ash suggest that how we conceive of heaven and hell determines how we live now? Do you agree? Why?

2 In the video, Professor Ash wonders if it is reasonable to think that each of us has an individual demonic tempter. This is an extracanonical point (meaning we don't find it in Scripture), but that does not mean it isn't worth considering. What do you think?

3 Why would it be wrong to suggest that the demonic forces of hell are competing with the heavenly powers of God? How does Christianity offer a more hopeful position than dualistic worldviews that understand good and evil as equally opposing parties in competition?

4 C. S. Lewis once suggested that there are two equal and opposing mistakes to make when it comes to thinking about devils: (1) to think they don't exist, and (2) to become overly fixated on them (see the preface to *The Screwtape Letters* for more). Which of these two errors do you think is more common today?

5 Professor Ash confesses that it took him some time for him to appreciate *The Screwtape Letters* when he first read it, but that it is now one of his favorite books. Why did he initially struggle with this work? Can you relate to this experience? What changed in Professor Ash or yourself, and how can that help us engage this book in a helpful way?

SECTION TWO

READING *THE SCREWTAPE LETTERS*

A s Professor Ash notes, *The Screwtape Letters* is broken up into 31 different letters, all of which concern a different issue or temptation ranging from human relations to reading theology to periods of emotional stagnation. While at first glance these letters appear to be written as evangelism for hell, they are actually evangelism for the life of heaven. By revealing the upside-down logic of sin and its effects on the human mind, C. S. Lewis designed these letters as a way to help humans see *through* the temptation we all face in our day-to-day lives.

But how can someone possibly write on such an unpopular topic—sin—and find a hungry audience for his work? The answer is found in Lewis's witty insights and satirical depiction of the logic of hell (seen in his ability to poke fun at hell while still providing thoughtful instruction) paired with his firsthand experience of temptation. When read rightly, *The Screwtape Letters* unveils the deathly reality lurking behind the lures of temptation and calls readers away from a God-deficient life into a fuller life with God.

In this section, Professor Ash focuses on several key insights from this work, including prayer (Letter 4), the law of undulation (Letter 8), the trend of "church shopping" (Letter 16), and gluttony (Letter 17).

PRAYER

In his discussion of Screwtape's approach to prayer, Professor Ash notes the problem of thinking we must *feel* a certain way or possess a certain mood in order for our prayers to be effective or proper. That is not at all the case. As Lewis insists, this sort of an understanding of prayer looks more like mental gymnastics than actual communion with God. What this understanding of prayer does is turn our focus from God toward ourselves, which is precisely the opposite of the point of prayer.

What is important in prayer is not our emotional response, but our communing with God, which may or may not involve an emotional component. Here, as elsewhere, Lewis is concerned with correcting a certain overemphasis on emotions perhaps even more apparent in our own day than his. The lesson to be gained from this consideration of prayer is that it often requires a great deal of practice and effort—not to control our emotions, but to constantly return our attention away from ourselves and toward the God who calls us to himself in prayer.

THE LAW OF UNDULATION

Professor Ash's greatest attention in this video is reserved for what Lewis calls the "law of undulation" (Letter 8). Like the college students Professor Ash has counseled, we all go through periods of difficult valleys as well as exciting peaks. The problem comes when we conclude that our spiritual struggles are a result of our own failures as Christians. While there may be instances in which our physical struggles result in spiritual struggles—for we are creatures with both body and soul, and the one is always related to the other—we cannot necessarily conclude that our spiritual struggles are a result of our own moral lapses or failures. We will have seasons where we are walking closely with the Lord—making regular time for prayer, treating others with the courtesy and love we are called to give them, and working "unto the Lord"—while feeling very distant from him, and we do not know why.

What is important to remember at such times, Professor Ash reminds us by way of Lewis's writing, is that these seasons come and go. What is important is our *obedience* to God, and not a particular emotional state. As Lewis puts it, we are "amphibians—half spirit and half animal," and it is only natural that life will involve a sort of undulation, or pattern of ups and downs. By knowing that such undulation is inevitable in life, we will be better prepared to face it. It is one of Christianity's many paradoxes that some of our greatest periods of spiritual growth will come in the most difficult periods of life. The mother who suffers the seemingly insurmountable loss of burying her own child will come to a kind of spiritual maturity she may not have otherwise reached. The same is true for the hardworking businessman who loses his job and is forced to rely on God in ways he has never had to before: it is in our greatest pain and loss that we come to know God most deeply. (C. S. Lewis discusses this again in his in his treatise on suffering, *The Problem of Pain.*)

We must not think that physical and material comforts are signs of a healthy walk with the Lord. The very opposite may be the case, as Screwtape suggests in Letter 18: "Whatever you do, keep your patient as safe as you possibly can."

CHURCH SHOPPING

Lewis spends much time in *The Screwtape Letters*—as he does elsewhere in his writing—poignantly portraying how temptation rears its ugly head in everyday church life. He points out an important but often-overlooked point: how easily we can be tempted away from God precisely in the place where we gather to draw near to God.

In Letter 16, Screwtape insists that Wormwood must put it into his patient's mind that what he really needs is to find the *right* church. This temptation is still alive and well today—whether it's an issue of finding "the right" music, preacher, or people— and more than a half century after they were originally penned, Lewis's insights in this letter are still as timely as they are helpful.

Lewis drew on his own experience with the church to show the ways in which temptation affects us in this setting. Using Screwtape's perspective, he shows that we are tempted to think that the deficiencies in those who are seated beside us on Sunday morning are linked to a greater deficiency in Christianity in general. We are led to think, "Do we actually believe this stuff?" by something as mundane as the hairstyle of the woman next to us or the voice of the man singing in the row behind us. By using satire, Lewis shows us not only the underlying humor of such scenarios, but also the very real, very powerful effect of temptation at work.

Professor Ash notes two important points that we can take away from this chapter. First, this consumerist approach to church attendance creates divisions, whereby we believe that since the church we attend is the church we chose, then it must be the best—and, as a result, all other churches are inferior. Rather than helping create a unified, universal church body—as described in our study of *Mere Christianity*—this attitude only fractures the church.

The second point is as basic as it is essential: since churches are made up of imperfect people, all churches will themselves be imperfect. This is an important point for any of us who are looking for the "perfect" church. There is no such thing. As long as we're looking for the "perfect" church, we will be disappointed. Of course, we only need to remind ourselves that if we ever *did* find "the perfect church," it likely wouldn't take us, with all our imperfections! We must also keep this in mind when we're looking for the "right" church.

GLUTTONY OF DELICACY

In another letter (Letter 17), Lewis deals with the sin of gluttony, but in a way we might not expect. Rather than talking about "gluttony of excess"—of gorging ourselves on food or material possessions, both of which are very real temptations—Lewis instead focuses on the temptation of "gluttony of delicacy." Lewis refers to this temptation as those who are trained in the "All-I-Want" mentality: These are the people whose meal is never *quite* right, who want something slightly different than what they have.

In the same way that those who gorge themselves on *too much* food have potentially made their stomachs the most important thing in their lives, those who fall to gluttony of delicacy also have an unhealthy focus, but in the opposite direction: for them, the issue is not *quantity*, but *quality*. And this temptation, though not often discussed, is alive and well today.

Boutique shops and restaurants serving artisan food and drinks are a thriving business in North America and elsewhere. Ever-increasing desires for higher-quality food and richer tastes are often seen as a sign of refinement to aspire to rather than as a temptation to be avoided. But in this letter, Lewis warns us that this should not be the case for Christians.

The reason Christians ought to shun such gluttony of delicacy, Professor Ash notes, is that when we allow anything besides the living God to run our lives, that thing becomes a problem. When I put my own preferences above the needs and hospitality of others, I've traded my commitment to loving God and loving others for love of my own tastes. As Professor Ash notes, these seemingly small requests or habits are actually the canary in the proverbial coal mine: gluttony of delicacy is often a sign of a bigger problem. In a very subtle way, the sin of gluttony of delicacy reveals the fact that something other than Christ is at the center of our life. And so those seemingly small requests can often lead us down a road that we do not want to go down, and which leads us, if we let it, to the place none of us actually desire: hell.

Lewis notes this point in a powerful way through the character of Screwtape. Writing to his young demon apprentice, Wormwood, Screwtape insists that he ought not focus on the "big" temptations, or the gigantic sins; the small sins will do the job: "Indeed the safest road to Hell is the gradual one" (Letter 12). The point Lewis is making here is that all of our choices are pointing is in one direction or another. And so the question we must always ask, at every possible fork in the road, is: *In which direction is this habit leading me?*

FOR REFLECTION

1 Professor Ash emphasizes the dangers of making our emotional response the focus of prayer, rather than obedience to and simply focusing on God. How do you focus on God in prayer, rather than on your own emotional state or response?

2 How can Lewis's lesson on the law of undulation help you interpret, understand, and even move forward when you're experiencing a particularly dry season of life?

3 Lewis points out the absurdity of thinking that the quirks of those at our church somehow mean Christianity is less plausible. This is an insightful as well as vulnerable point. Can you relate to this temptation? How is Lewis's reminder that there are no perfect churches helpful?

4 How is gluttony of delicacy an even more dangerous sin than gluttony of excess? In your experience, has the church dealt with one more than the other? Why do you think that is? What makes Lewis's description of this kind of gluttony helpful?

CONCLUDING
THE SCREWTAPE LETTERS

W HILE THERE ARE 31 CHAPTERS IN *THE SCREWTAPE LETTERS*, we are only able to focus on a handful of Screwtape's letters in this study. In this final section of the episode, Professor Ash discusses a last handful of important themes, including the question of whether Satan could ever be let back into heaven; how birth prepares us for death; and the essentially selfish nature of hell. We will reflect on each of these three points in turn.

SATAN'S FINAL STATE

In Letter 19, C. S. Lewis writes from the hellish perspective on the reason why Satan was thrown out of heaven—which is, of course, the opposite of how Christians have understood the story. Rather than being forcibly removed from heaven, Screwtape insists that Satan *chose* to remove himself from the presence of God because of "an unprovoked lack of confidence" in Satan. Ultimately, C. S. Lewis suggests that the real reason Satan was banished from heaven was because he could not understand love. Due to his own pride, Satan could not receive the love God created him to receive and live into as God's creature. Rather than embrace this relationship of creator-creature love—a relationship of dependency—Satan desired to overthrow, overpower, or actually to *be* God. As a result, Satan was banished from God's presence, as Lewis puts it, because Satan could not understand the meaning and reality of divine love.

The same is true for the demons in *The Screwtape Letters,* who cannot comprehend the fact that God actually, truly loves humans. It is their misunderstanding—their inability to understand the reality of divine love—that has led to their expulsion from God's presence. In an interesting way, Lewis concludes that there remains the possibility that Satan will one day learn the lesson of divine love and choose to live into it, thereby being allowed to return to his original heavenly state: "Members of His [God's] faction have frequently admitted that if ever we came to understand what He means by love, the war would be over and we should re-enter Heaven" (Letter 19). Twentieth-century Catholic theologian Hans Urs von Balthasar supported Lewis's suggestion that there remains the possibility of even Satan ultimately being in heaven in his book, *Dare We Hope,* where he writes that "the church which has sanctified so many men, has never said anything about the damnation of any individual".[2]

Lewis makes an interesting point regarding Satan's final state. While there are biblical references to Satan's removal from heaven (e.g., Luke 10:18; Isa 14:12–14; Ezek 28:12–18), much of our thought on Satan's heavenly banishment and final state are extracanonical speculation—they come from tradition outside of what Scripture reveals to us. It's worth asking, though, how Lewis's depiction of the possibility of Satan being returned to heaven shapes and informs our own understanding of heaven and hell. If we believed it possible that any and all creatures—even Satan himself—could be redeemed and reunited with God, would we treat them differently?

BIRTH AS PREPARATION FOR DEATH

In Letter 28, Screwtape suggests that the point of every human birth is death: "It is obvious that to Him human birth is important chiefly as the qualification for human death, and death solely as the gate to that other kind of life." As Professor Ash notes, this is one point where the demon gets it right: "If you think about it, of all the things that a birth can produce as a life goes on ... the thing that matters the most in a life where there has been birth and the life goes on is whether one is ready for death." Birth and all of our earthly life, according to Lewis, are preparation for death. And, in that way, they are preparation for *real* life.

While Scripture certainly seems to present our eternal life with God as of utmost importance, the danger of teaching that the point of life is death is that the significance of earthly life and experiences can be downplayed. If we are not careful, by focusing too much on heavenly life, earthly life can be ignored. Of course, the equal and opposite mistake can also be made: by focusing so much on earthly life, we can come to ignore the importance of heavenly life. While losing sight of the importance of earthly life for the sake of heavenly life does not appear to be the mistake Lewis is making here or elsewhere, it's worth noting so that we can avoid either error.

The appropriate Christian posture is one that holds both views in balance: earthly life matters, heavenly life matters more.

And what Lewis is saying here, in the voice of Screwtape in *The Screwtape Letters*, is helpful for keeping the two in balance. Note that Screwtape encourages his apprentice Wormwood to do everything in his power to keep the patient alive, so that, in time, he might win the patient "by attrition" of his soul (Letter 18). The demons take seriously the formative nature of our earthly life. So, too, should we. By understanding our earthly life as training for heavenly life, we are encouraged to take our earthly life *more* seriously, not less. The reason is that now, more than ever, each and every choice we make, every action we take, and, indeed, everything that we are involved in is shaping us in important ways, not just for 70, 80, or 90 years, but for all of eternity. This fits with what Lewis has to say elsewhere, in *Mere Christianity*: "All your life long you are slowly turning this central thing [in yourself] either into a heavenly creature or into a hellish creature" (Chapter 7, Book 3, *Mere Christianity*).

THE SELFISH NATURE OF HELL

In the final chapter of *The Screwtape Letters*, the reader celebrates the death of the patient and his entrance into heavenly life. The glory and brilliance and joy of the patient's heavenly transition is something Screwtape and Wormwood simply cannot comprehend (see Letter 31).

Just as interesting as Lewis's depiction of the mysterious point of the patient's entrance into the heavenly realm is how Screwtape replies to this "failure" on Wormwood's part: his response is one of anger that the patient is now enjoying his new life in the full presence of God. However, Screwtape finds satisfaction in Wormwood's failure, precisely because it means his own benefit:

"I think they will give you to me now; or a bit of you. Love you? Why, yes. As dainty a morsel as ever I grew fat on" (Letter 31). Now that Wormwood has failed his mission, Screwtape reveals his plan to quite literally devour his young apprentice. One demon's failure is another demon's gain. And so it is the essentially selfish nature of hell, as depicted by Lewis.

What does this have to say to us? In a potentially surprising way, Lewis's description of the nature of hell can reflect our own relationships back to us—forcing us to examine what's at the core of our relationships. For many of us, even many Christians, our relationships are utilitarian in nature: we spend time and make time for those who have something to offer us. As Professor Ash notes, hellish creatures want to bring others into their lives so that they can grow at others' expense. Similarly, we love those who give us something for our own gain. And when those people cease to have something to offer us, we suddenly find we have less time for them—we rid ourselves of them. This is, as Lewis is showing in an imaginative way, characteristic of relationships in hell—not heaven.

The Bible depicts a different picture of how our relationships should look. For Christians, others have value not from what they offer us, but simply because they are image-bearers of God, created as God's beloved children, and reflecting God himself back to us. I gain merely from being around you, no matter your income or career or status, because by being in your presence, I am experiencing a glimpse of God's own image. Your differences from me reflect the divine qualities of God in a way that I need. And my life is made more heavenly by those who are unlike me, those who have nothing to offer me but their time, their presence, and their own divine image. And when I realize that, I begin to glimpse something of the heavenly picture of human relations.

FOR REFLECTION

1 What do you think of Lewis leaving the door open for Satan's redemption and return to his original heavenly state? How does this sort of optimism affect how we think about the evil in our own world?

2 Why does Lewis suggest that life is preparation for death? Does this make our earthly life less important? How are we to keep a heavenward gaze while maintaining a deep appreciation and care for the matters of earthly life?

3 The final correspondence of *The Screwtape Letters* is both celebratory—the patient is now moving heavenward—and horrific—Screwtape is preparing to devour his apprentice, Wormwood. Wormwood's failure is an opportunity for Screwtape's own benefit. How does this depiction of demonic relations reflect some human relations? What do heaven-informed relationships look like, in contrast?

THE PROBLEM OF PAIN

DID YOU KNOW?

Lewis initially requested that his name not be used on *The Problem of Pain*, as he thought readers would laugh at the idea of a privileged Oxford don writing on such a topic. In the end, Lewis was persuaded to use his name on the book, and he explained his reservations in the preface.

Curiously, in an early advertisement for *The Problem of Pain* in *The Church Times* of 1949, Lewis's name was listed as "C. S. Lewis, M.D."

C. S. Lewis wrote a preface to the French edition of *The Problem of Pain* that was unique from the English version. In it, Lewis offers an extended version of his interest in "mere" Christianity (those aspects of the Christian faith that unite believers) rather than issues of controversy, which he prefers to leave to "the business of theologians."

SECTION ONE

LEWIS'S FIRST
APOLOGETIC WRITING

F OR MOST OF US WHO ARE FAMILIAR WITH C. S. LEWIS'S WRIT-
ing, the word "apologist" comes to mind. Lewis is well known
today for his clear, thoughtful defense and articulation of the
Christian faith. But that wasn't always so; in *The Problem of Pain*,
we see C. S. Lewis's first work of Christian apologetic writing.
Specifically, Lewis is examining the age-old question, "If God is
good, then why do bad things happen?" As Professor Ash notes,
Lewis doesn't avoid difficult issues—genocide, torture, and natural disasters are all part of our tragic history and present reality, and here, in *The Problem of Pain*, they are faced head-on from
a Christian perspective.

For many years, this question was one of the biggest obstacles
preventing Lewis from faith in God. In *The Problem of Pain*, we not
only see a believing Christian examining pain and suffering in
light of a good, all-powerful God; we also see the other side of the
argument and look at the doubts Lewis wrestled with while still
an atheist. For example, Lewis writes in the Introduction to *The*

Problem of Pain: "If the universe is so bad, or even half so bad, how on earth did human beings ever come to attribute it to the activity of a wise and good Creator?" This question that C. S. Lewis would have wrestled with as a young atheist so many years earlier echoes another, similar argument made elsewhere, in *Mere Christianity*: that in trying to explain where humans come by their sense of justice, atheism "turns out to be too simple" (Book 1, Chapter 1, *Mere Christianity*).

In *The Problem of Pain*, we have front-row tickets to one of the great minds of the past century wrestling with one of the biggest questions facing humanity while drawing on years spent thinking through the intricacies of this issue as both an atheist *and* as a Christian. Let us follow along not so that we might add noise to the many debates on this topic, but in hopes that we might help others grow close to God in the midst of the tragic pain and suffering that is as real today as it was during Lewis's time.

FOR REFLECTION

1 Pain is an inevitable reality of life. Some of us seem to have the misfortune of experiencing more of it than others, but all of us taste its bitterness in one way or another. Think about those you know who are going through a particularly difficult period right now. Keep them in mind as we go through this study, paying attention to anything said that might be helpful for them, and how you might carefully introduce it to them in a helpful, thoughtful way.

2 What Bible passages come to mind when you think of pain and suffering? What does Scripture have to say about suffering in the Christian life? What is our response supposed to be? Why? Keep these Scripture texts in mind throughout this study, and see how they fit with what Lewis teaches on this topic.

3 Why is the problem of pain not simply a problem for Christians? Why do atheists have to account for this issue as well?

AN OUTLINE OF
THE PROBLEM OF PAIN

*T*HE PROBLEM OF PAIN CONSISTS OF 10 CHAPTERS, RANGING FROM a discussion of God's omnipotence and how this relates to the suffering in this world, to the fall of man, hell, animal pain, and heaven, among other topics. What Lewis presents in this book is the Christian response to the issue of pain, which he argues is not simply a response that arose from human minds, but which is a matter of revelation from God. If what Christianity offered was simply one more human argument, attempting to make sense of the suffering in this world, it would be of no more worth to us than any other argument. But, if the Christian response to the problem of pain is the revelation of God, derived not from human minds but from God's word, then we must pay close attention to what is being said. We must take great care to understand Lewis's teaching on this point—not so that we can win an argument or a debate, but so that we can better navigate the complexities of pain and suffering in our lives as well as in others' lives.

In this video, Professor Ash offers a broad analysis of Lewis's book, *The Problem of Pain*, which seeks to make sense of the tragic pain and evil in our world along with the belief in a good God. Without merely repeating Professor Ash's teaching, we will pay special attention to what he highlights from Lewis's work, while also attending to those aspects of this book that Ash spends less time on, such as the issue of animal pain. We will begin with the question of God's omnipotence.

FREE WILL AND THE LIMITS OF GOD'S POWER

C. S. Lewis offers a helpful response to a common question about evil in the world: If God is all powerful, then why doesn't he do something about evil? Some readers will be shocked by Lewis's response: there are some things that are impossible for God—not because of a limit in God's power, but simply because they are *intrinsically* impossible.

The question of evil, offered as a critique of God's existence or power, isn't so much a question of God's power, but a nonsensical statement. For example, to ask whether God could create something so heavy that God could not lift it is not an argument against God's omnipotence, but an instance of nonsensical logic. And that is often what we run into in regards to the question of God's omnipotence: "It is no more possible for God than for the weakest of His creatures to carry out both of two mutually exclusive alternatives; not because His power meets an obstacle, but because nonsense remains nonsense even when we talk it about God" (Chapter 2, *The Problem of Pain*). In asking questions about the limits of God's power, we must carefully consider whether the question's premise is actually a limitation or whether it's nonsense. And this has important implications for our understanding of suffering in this world, particularly as it relates to human free will.

Central to Lewis's argument for the existence of pain and suffering in the world is his insistence that God created humanity with the agency to choose either good or evil. Once this choice was introduced, there remained the possibility for pain. The suffering we see on the news and in our own lives is not an argument against God; it is a natural result of God giving humanity the choice to do good or to do evil.

But why would God give humans such a choice if it meant all of the tragic pain and suffering that has plagued human history? As Lewis notes in *Mere Christianity*: "Free will, though it makes evil possible, is also the only thing that makes possible any love or goodness or joy worth having" (Chapter 3, Book 2, *Mere Christianity*). The first humans were created with the freedom to choose good or to do evil. They chose the latter, and so too have all those who came after them. God existed in a self-sufficient state of love for all eternity (1 John 4:8; Ps 90:2; Rev 1:8), but out of this gratuitous, overflowing love, he created humanity to share in this love. However, God was not interested in creating robots who were forced to receive this love, Lewis explains. Without having the ability to choose God, humans' ability to receive God's love would make true love impossible.

And so, says Lewis, "Of course God knew what would happen if they used their freedom the wrong way: apparently He thought it worth the risk" (Chapter 3, Book 2, *Mere Christianity*). The biblical view of creation suggests that human free will was necessary. But once free will was possible, then suffering was possible, too. We could argue with God's decision to create humans that had the potential to choose evil, given all the suffering that has resulted from this choice, but, as Lewis points out, there is a problem with arguing with God—God is the one who created our ability to reason and argue in the first place!

Lewis goes on in Chapter 2 of *The Problem of Pain* to note that the world we live in is a stable world with a nature that obeys certain laws. Were God to intervene and prevent any and all instances in which our free will resulted in evil, then our world would be a very unstable world indeed, one in which we could not have order in any real sense, and free will would become void.

FOR REFLECTION

1 Why does C. S. Lewis argue that there are some things that are impossible for God? Can you give an example? Why is this helpful to consider when it comes to the problem of pain?

2 Why is it important to think about free will for the problem of pain? Why does Lewis suggest we cannot argue for free will without also expecting pain and suffering? Why does he suggest God gave humanity free will in the first place?

3 When discussing the problem of pain with those who are currently or who have undergone deeply painful experiences in the past, how can this conversation be introduced in a helpful way that doesn't merely feel like an intellectual exercise?

DIVINE GOODNESS: GOD'S LOVE ≠ MERE KINDNESS

In discussing the second chapter of *The Problem of Pain*, Professor Ash notes Lewis's important distinction between God's love and mere kindness. As he points out, many questions concerning God's goodness, such as when people ask, "How could a good God allow...?", are not actually questions of God's goodness, but are a misunderstanding between love and mere kindness.

What most of us have not fully grasped when it comes to this question of divine goodness is the reality that God loves us. God loves his creation. Do not miss the significance of this point; that is remarkable! God loves humanity, even in its brokenness. And that love is a *genuine* love, a wish for our well-being from a heavenly point of view that sees the world and us in it in ways we simply cannot. Lewis clarifies this distinction when he says that, by "goodness," God means love, whereas humans most often mean simply being nice (see Chapter 3, *The Problem of Pain*). Lewis notes that divine love is "something more stern and splendid than mere kindness ... He [God] has paid us the intolerable compliment of loving us, in the deepest, most tragic, and inexorable sense." In order to help explain this point, Professor Ash offers several helpful illustrations from Lewis's work that clarify this distinction between God's love for humanity and what is more properly understood as kindness. The first illustration is that of an artist and his masterpiece. In order for this work to truly be a masterpiece, the artist will not simply create it once and then leave it; he will continue to refine and maintain it in order to make it perfect. That's his goal, after all: not "good enough," but perfection. The same is true of our Creator. As Jesus taught in the Sermon on the Mount, "You therefore must be perfect, as your heavenly Father is perfect" (Matt 5:48).

Of course, as Professor Ash notes, if this work of art were not a nonsentient slab of marble or a canvas but instead a living being, as we are alive, then it would not likely sit by and remain silent while the artist works away. Instead, it would likely have an opinion on all the work—perhaps even questioning whether this work was actually necessary. If the artist's goal were just a "nice" painting, then this work would not be necessary. But if the artist's goal is perfection—as our Lord's goal is for us—then this work, painstaking though it may be, is absolutely vital. (See Chapter 9, Book 4 of *Mere Christianity* for another take on this idea.)

In response to the question of how we can believe in a good, loving God in the face of pervasive suffering in the world, C. S. Lewis concludes: "The problem of reconciling human suffering with the existence of a God who loves, is only insoluble so long as we attach a trivial meaning to the word 'love.'" What must be understood, Lewis emphasizes, is that God's love for humanity is not mere niceness. God's love for humanity is a love that desires our best interests—that desires, indeed, our perfection.

If God's goal for our lives were merely to make us "good," then the Christian life would be much easier. The fact that it is not—our own Lord urges us to "count the cost" before picking up our cross and following him (Luke 14:25-33)—should encourage us that God is at work in our lives, particularly in the deepest, darkest valleys, molding us more and more into the image of his Son, Jesus Christ. And in that reminder, we ought to find comfort, joy, and hope.

FOR REFLECTION

1 In reflecting on the glaring reality of pain and suffering in our world, Lewis notes, "Since I have reason to believe...that God is Love, I conclude that my conception of love needs correction" (Chapter 3, *The Problem of Pain*). Why is this a helpful response to those who ask, "If God is good, then why do bad things happen?"

2 Do you find the illustration of God as an artist and humans as his masterpiece to be helpful in interpreting the challenges, pain, and even suffering in your own life? How?

3   Professor Ash explained the difference between divine goodness/love and mere niceness with several illustrations: the relationship between an animal and the animal's master, a father and son, and a husband and wife. Did you find any of these illustrations particularly helpful? Did you find any of them unhelpful or confusing? Why?

4   Why might it not be helpful to tell others that the pain they are experiencing is God's work?

C. S. LEWIS'S LIFE

DID YOU KNOW?

Though he spent most of his life in England, C. S. Lewis was born in Belfast, Ireland, on November 29, 1898.

C. S. Lewis was the younger of two children. His older brother, Major Warren "Warnie" Lewis, retired from the military and also became an accomplished writer.

Lewis was baptized in the Church of Ireland on January 29, 1899.

As a young boy, C. S. Lewis dreamed of being a published author one day. However, his initial aspirations were for poetry.

Lewis served in England's forces during World War I. He was badly injured in battle and managed to recover away from enemy lines— an experience that may have saved his life.

C. S. Lewis did not become widely recognized for his writing until his 30s, after his Christian conversion.

An atheist from his teenage years through his early 30s, Lewis initially became theist and only later Christian.

Most of Lewis's adult years were spent as a bachelor. He was nearly sixty years old when he first married his wife, Joy, an American from New York.

C. S. Lewis's face appeared on the cover of *Time* magazine in 1947. The September 8 cover article was titled, "His Heresy: Christianity."

Though most of his academic career was spent teaching English Language and Literature at Oxford University, Lewis retired from Cambridge University after nearly a decade as the Chair of Medieval and Renaissance Literature (1954–1963). Interestingly, he went from teaching at Magdalen College, Oxford, to Magdalene College, Cambridge.

C. S. Lewis passed away on November 22, 1963, one week from his sixty-fifth birthday, and the same day US President John F. Kennedy was assassinated. It was also the same day Aldous Huxley, author of *A Brave New World,* died.

Though he never earned a doctoral degree in a traditional sense, Lewis received honorary doctoral degrees, including from the University of Manchester, the University of Dijon, and the University of St. Andrews.

At the time of his passing, Lewis had authored more than 30 books; more were published posthumously.

LEWIS'S EARLY DAYS

A<small>S PROFESSOR TONY ASH INTRODUCES AT THE OUTSET OF THIS</small> video, though C. S. Lewis is most often referred to as an English writer and Oxford don, he was actually born in Belfast, Ireland, in 1898. He did, however, spend most of his life in England.

THE LEWIS FAMILY

C. S. Lewis was raised in an upper-middle class home in Northern Ireland, to two church-going Protestant parents, Albert and Flora Lewis.

Albert was a solicitor, or a government law officer, who loved books. He was incredibly well read; some biographers have even gone so far as to suggest that Albert's legal profession was merely a way to pay for his true literary passion. Whatever the case may be, there is no denying that Albert's success in the law room was due to his passionate oratory skills; he was a gifted public speaker. At the family home, Albert loved telling stories to Lewis and his brother, Warren, or any guests who were present.

Lewis's mother, Flora, was exceptionally gifted in mathematics. A pioneer for women in academics, Flora earned first class honors in logic and second class honors in mathematics at what is now Queen's University in Belfast, before the turn of the twentieth century. She did not, it seems, pass along her mathematical skills to her youngest son. Flora's father—C. S. Lewis's maternal grandfather—was a Protestant pastor with great rhetorical talent. And, like her husband, Flora was described as a voracious reader. As a result, Lewis's childhood home was a literary treasure trove, never short on new stories.

C. S. Lewis's older brother, who went by Warnie, was three years older than Lewis and was his closest friend for most of his life.

MUCH TIME INDOORS

In his autobiography *Surprised By Joy*, Lewis talks about spending much of his childhood indoors due to the wet Irish weather, which meant much of his childhood was spent reading and writing books. From an early age, Lewis and his brother wrote incredibly detailed accounts of fictional lands, complete with geography, political systems, and complex characters.

Perhaps most interesting about Boxen—the name for Lewis's childhood literary world—is that it was inhabited by animals who could talk and who wore human clothes. Very early on, we see hints of the imagination that would influence his later work.

"JACK"

Though he was born Clive Staples Lewis, and though most who know him through his writing refer to him as C. S. Lewis, he actually was called "Jack" from a very young age by most of his close friends and family.

This nickname came from a pet dog, which his family owned when Lewis was young. Apparently the dog, named "Jaxie," was struck by a car when Lewis was just a boy. Distraught by the news, Lewis returned home one day declaring that from that day forward, he would be known as "Jaxie." That name was later shortened to "Jax," which became "Jack," the name Lewis went by with his close friends and family for the remainder of his life.

JOY

It was also during this period in his life that Lewis claimed to have his first experience of the transcendental, in several unexpected ways.

Stuck inside for much of his youth by the inclement Irish weather, Lewis wrote (in *Surprised by Joy*) of watching the rolling emerald hills on the horizon from the windows of his childhood home and being struck by pains of joy—a longing for that which was always beyond his reach.

On another occasion, Warnie brought Lewis a biscuit-tin lid, covered in moss, with little twigs done up to resemble a miniature garden. For reasons that perhaps were not even clear to C. S. Lewis, this brought the young Lewis great joy, the memory of which stayed with him for the rest of his life.

Though Lewis uses the English word "joy" to describe these experiences, he points out that the German word *Sehnsucht* is more fitting—it describes a sort of joy that includes longing, a joy that points beyond the immediate experience. Lewis describes this feeling as "an unsatisfied desire, which is itself more satisfying than any other desire." This theme—insisting that what we see is not all there is to be seen, that our deepest joys lie somehow beyond the world we know and experience—would later be important for Lewis's spiritual journey.

TWO DEEP PAINS

Lewis suffered two difficult experiences early on in his life, which had a powerful impact on him, including his faith, for many years to come.

Before he was ten years old, Lewis's mother became quite ill. The doctors found cancer, and Lewis found himself praying for his mother's recovery. Those prayers ultimately went unanswered, however, and Lewis lost his mother before his tenth birthday. "All that was tranquil and reliable disappeared from my life," C. S. Lewis writes of this period in his life.

Within just a few weeks of losing his mother, Lewis's father shipped Lewis off to school in England. Already mourning the loss of his mother at such a young age, Lewis was now missing the only home he had ever known while adjusting to a new, foreign country. This was, according to Lewis, one of the darkest periods of his life.

In light of such pains at such an early age, it should not be surprising that the young Lewis began to lose faith in the Christianity in which he had been raised.

KIRKPATRICK

Another contribution to Lewis's turning his back on the Christian faith of his childhood was the influence of his private tutor, Kirkpatrick. Previously a Protestant minister when he was

Lewis's father's school headmaster, Kirkpatrick was an atheist by the time fifteen-year-old C. S. Lewis came for private tutorials. While Kirkpatrick's role as private tutor was to help prepare the young Lewis for the Oxford entrance exams, his influence can be seen in several important ways.

First, in the area of logic: Kirkpatrick brought a razor-sharp appreciation for logic to Lewis's thought, which was still present in his writing many years later. Kirkpatrick held a high regard for reason, for thoughtful speech, and for thinking carefully before speaking even the most commonplace sentences. "I didn't expect it to look like this," the young Lewis commented shortly after stepping off the train and greeting his new tutor. After being asked by Kirkpatrick why he would have reason to think his new home would look any different than it did, and after realizing he had no good reason to think it would look otherwise, Lewis was encouraged not to make statements that had no supportable basis. Such an approach to logic and speech stuck with Lewis.

In addition, Kirkpatrick is the one who first sensed Lewis's prodigious talent for literary criticism, predicting Lewis's future success in this area in a letter to Lewis's father. "It is the maturity and originality of his literary judgments which is so unusual and surprising," Kirkpatrick wrote to Albert Lewis. "By an unerring instinct he detects first rate quality in literary workmanship and the second rate does not interest him in any way."[1] Kirkpatrick encouraged Lewis in this area, and under his tutelage, Lewis honed his literary talent.

Lastly, while Lewis likely was already settling into atheism by the time he arrived at Kirkpatrick's home, his tutor's ardent atheism only solidified Lewis's position. Of particular influence was a book Kirkpatrick appreciated greatly and which Lewis read at the time: *The Golden Bough*. A highly popular book on comparative religion published at the time Lewis was studying under Kirkpatrick (1914–17), J. G. Frazer's *The Golden Bough* argues that all of the world's religions and folklore are really, at bottom, made of the same common themes. In this way, he argues, Christianity is nothing new, but simply one more human attempt to explain the world and humans' role in it. This idea would quickly become a cornerstone of Lewis's atheism, as we can see in note he wrote to his childhood friend, Arthur Greeves, at the time: "All religion, that is, all mythologies to give them their proper name, are merely man's own invention—Christ as much as Loki" (October 12, 1916, published in *They Stand Together*).[2]

FOR REFLECTION

1 The question of how a good God can allow evil to occur to his beloved creation is a question that we have seen Lewis address in previous episodes of our study. Here, in this biographical consideration of Lewis's life, we see that this was not an abstract question for Lewis, but was a profound reality for him at a young age. How might Lewis's experience of losing his mother after praying for her recovery have resulted not only in his departure from the Christian faith of his youth, but also impacted his return to and articulation of the Christian faith?

2 Lewis was struck by several early experiences that pointed him beyond simply the world we can see and touch, experiences that would be vital to his eventual return to Christianity. What experiences from your own childhood pointed you toward God?

SECTION TWO

PHANTASTES, WORLD WAR I,
AND LEWIS'S CONVERSION

GEORGE MACDONALD'S *PHANTASTES*

While several experiences arguably led C. S. Lewis to walk away from the Christian faith in which he was raised, it was in reading George MacDonald's fantasy novel *Phantastes* (1858), on March 4, 1916, that Lewis later recounts having his imagination "baptized." In 1962, *The Christian Century* asked C. S. Lewis to list the books that most shaped his "vocational attitude and [his] philosophy of life." At the start of the list was *Phantastes*. Even though he was then an atheist, Lewis wrote that it was in MacDonald's fiction that he found a work which "had about it a sort of cool, morning innocence ... What it actually did to me was to convert, even to baptize ... my imagination" (*George MacDonald: An Anthology*). Indeed, in his autobiography, *Surprised by Joy*, Lewis writes: "That night my imagination was, in a certain sense, baptized; the rest of me, not unnaturally, took longer. I had not the faintest notion what I had let myself in for by buying *Phantastes*" (Chapter 11, *Surprised by Joy*).

Even though it would take Lewis nearly fifteen years to return to Christianity, Lewis's mind already was seeing how the common things of life and reality could be illumined by the divine presence that lies beyond that which we can see and touch.

WORLD WAR I

Even though Lewis was not required to enter the British military, given his Irish birth, he voluntarily entered the service, considering it his duty. It was there, in his training before being sent off to the First World War—or the "Great War," as it was then called—that he met a young man by the name of Paddy Moore. The two men soon became friends. Shortly after meeting in training, the two men realized they had something rather important in common: both men had one parent and one sibling for family. While Lewis had lost his mother when he was just nine years old, Paddy Moore's family consisted of his mother—deserted by her husband—and his younger sister, Maureen.

Before leaving for battle, the two made a pact: *If one of us should not return from the war alive, the other should look after that man's family.* So these men left for the war with this agreement. Lewis was later injured in battle, hit by a piece of shrapnel that sent him to a hospital, where he was able to recover away from enemy lines. His friend Paddy Moore, however, was not so lucky; he did not return from battle alive.

When Lewis returned to Oxford to begin his studies, he moved in with Paddy Moore's family. Lewis and the two women—

Mrs. Janie Moore and Maureen—lived in several homes in and around Oxford while Lewis completed his degrees and began teaching at Oxford before they finally settled into the home in which Lewis would spend the majority of his adult years: the Kilns.

THE KILNS: LEWIS'S HOME FROM 1930-63

In 1930, C. S. Lewis moved into the home where he would spend the rest of his adult life. Lewis's father, Albert Lewis, passed away in 1929; after some discussion with his brother Warnie, Lewis decided that the money from the sale of their childhood home in Belfast would be used, along with some savings Mrs. Moore offered, to purchase the Kilns in Oxford in 1930.

When they first moved in, it was just Lewis and the two Moore women residing in the Kilns. Later, when he retired from the military, Lewis's brother, Warnie, joined them. Lewis and Warnie were brothers, of course, but they were also best friends; this move brought Lewis great joy. While the brothers had grown apart for many years, they were now reunited, enjoying rich conversation and their work in their common living space, something they had not enjoyed since they were children.

Lewis's home was called the Kilns because beside the home stood two large beehive-shaped towers, which were kilns where bricks had been fired before Lewis moved into the home. The home originally wasn't intended to be anything special when it was built in 1922; it was built simply as a place for the stone workers to live. Just behind the home is a large pond where these workers dredged clay and then used it to make bricks in the kilns.

So when Lewis bought the home in 1930, he not only bought the home but also eight acres of undeveloped property, including the pond and woods. Lewis loved to be outdoors, going for walks and enjoying the reprieve from the busyness of the Oxford city center and academic life.

But it was a very peculiar thing, Lewis living in this country home with these two women. In fact, this living arrangement would have been unheard of at the turn of the twentieth century: it's only been within the past 100 years or so that Oxford professors have even been allowed to be married. Prior to this change, it was expected that you lived at college and were completely devoted to your research, your writing, and your students. Life for an Oxford don was rather monastic.

But Lewis's life was very different from the stereotypical ivory-tower lifestyle of his colleagues. Even though Lewis had rooms provided for him at the college, where he could eat all of his meals, he chose to live three miles away, in the small village of Risinghurst—and this had a profound impact on his writing. Lewis would have been familiar with common domestic duties in a way many of his Oxford colleagues were not. At the Kilns, Lewis helped out with chores like taking care of the chickens, washing dishes, and attending to Mrs. Moore in her old age. This is a point many biographers miss about Lewis's life and writing: this domestic experience at the Kilns helped make Lewis's writing more relatable to the general public. Even more importantly, it was while living at the Kilns that Lewis became a Christian.

FROM ATHEISM TO THEISM, AND FROM THEISM TO CHRISTIANITY

Many people know that C. S. Lewis became a Christian as an adult atheist, but what many people miss is that he didn't move straight from atheism to Christianity. Instead, Lewis describes his conversion experience in *Surprised by Joy* as a two-step process: First, from atheism to theism (or belief in a God/god); and, second, from theism to Christianity. This all happened between 1930 and 1931.

In the first instance, Lewis describes himself as "the most reluctant convert in all of England," being pursued by God until he finally went from believing that there was no God to believing "that God is God and I am not" in the spring of 1930. Lewis was, in his early thirties, a theist.

But though Lewis believed in God at that point, and even while he began attending chapel services in Oxford at Magdalen College, he was not yet ready to believe Jesus was the Christ. That conversion took more time.

Specifically, that change didn't happen until the fall of 1931. On September 19, 1931, Lewis invited two of his Christian friends— J. R. R. Tolkien, who was then the Rawlinson and Bosworth Professor of Anglo-Saxon at Oxford University, as well as another close friend, Hugo Dyson, then a lecturer at the University of Reading—to join him for dinner at Magdalen College. The three men discussed myth and metaphor for much of the evening, and the focus of the conversation came to rest on Lewis's great pleasure in myths of the dying god: of the god who would sacrifice himself to himself, or who dies only later to revive (for example, in the stories of Balder, Adonis, and Bacchus), but only insofar as such myths stopped short of the Christian Gospels.

In a letter to his childhood friend Arthur Greeves that he had written just weeks earlier, Lewis noted the great myth of resurrection as portrayed in the story of Hermione in Shakespeare's *The Winter's Tale*: "I must confess that more and more the value of plays and novels becomes for me dependent on the moments when, by whatever artifice, they succeed in expressing the great myths.' "[3] Lewis loved such myths, but once they began to approach an explicit connection to Christianity, he wanted nothing to do with them. Pressing Lewis on this point, Tolkien and Dyson insisted that what he was not understanding was that in the Christian Gospels, one found all of these great myths becoming actual history in the person of Jesus. This conversation was perhaps the pivotal point in Lewis's return to Christianity.

Only nine days later, Lewis found himself traveling in the sidecar of his brother's motorcycle. It was during this trip that Lewis returned to faith in Christ as the Son of God, as he told Greeves in a letter on October 1, 1931: "I have just passed on from believing in God to definitely believing in Christ—in Christianity ... My long night talk with Dyson and Tolkien had a good deal to do with it."

When he left for the zoo in the sidecar of Warnie's motorcycle that day, Lewis said, he didn't believe Jesus was the divine Lord incarnate. When he returned, he did. The moment of Lewis's conversion is fairly anticlimactic as he describes it in *Surprised by Joy*, but it created a dramatic change in Lewis's life—especially in his writing. It wasn't until *after* his conversion to Christianity that Lewis's writing began to find widespread, popular success.

FOR REFLECTION

1 Why was reading George MacDonald's *Phantastes* such an important experience in Lewis's life? What difference did it make for his atheist worldview at the time of its reading?

2   What is the significance of Lewis's experience living at the Kilns? What are some of the reasons this would have been a peculiar arrangement, and what difference might this have had for his writing?

3   C. S. Lewis went from being an atheist to a theist, and then later from a theist to a Christian in a relatively short time. What difference did Lewis's late-night conversation with J. R. R. Tolkien and Hugo Dyson make in his perspective on Christianity? What does it mean to suggest that Christianity is a "myth become fact," as Lewis would later put it?

SECTION THREE

WORLD-FAMOUS CHRISTIAN APOLOGIST

LEWIS'S WRITINGS: 1930-40

The first book Lewis wrote and published after his conversion is titled *The Pilgrim's Regress* (1933); the book is a play on John Bunyan's classic allegory, *The Pilgrim's Progress*, and is an imaginary retelling of Lewis's own conversion experience—and, specifically, Lewis's search for what he refers to as "joy," and how this journey led him to Christianity. This book, which Lewis penned in only two weeks, also deals with the relationship between imagination and reason in his conversion—two important themes Lewis would wrestle with for many years.

While Lewis was later quite critical of the work—telling readers not to bother with it, as it was unnecessarily cumbersome—*The Pilgrim's Regress* began what would be Lewis's literary success.

Lewis's next book was *The Allegory of Love* (1936), an exploration of the allegorical treatment of love in the Middle Ages. That might seem like a strange time period to focus on for a book on this topic, but it made sense for Lewis—his Oxford teaching and research on literature focused on the Middle Ages. *The Allegory of Love* is a strong work academically; it's still used in literature classrooms to this day.

Lewis then wrote an apologetic work, *The Problem of Pain* (1940), in which he attempted to pose an answer to the question, *if God is good, then why do bad things happen?* Or, to put it another way: *God can be benevolent or omnipotent, but not both.* This question had been personally troubling to Lewis during his years as an atheist, and so here we see Lewis offering personal counsel from his own struggles with questions of pain. It was the publication of this book, however, that would open the door for what would become one of Lewis's most well-known Christian writings: *Mere Christianity*.

C. S. LEWIS THE WORLD-FAMOUS APOLOGIST: 1940S WRITINGS

The Problem of Pain caught the attention of Rev. James Welch, the director of religious broadcasting at the BBC. He wrote Lewis to ask if he might be willing to write a series of radio talks on Christian beliefs from the point of view of a layman. World War II had broken out across Europe and, as happens during times of war, people typically uninterested in God suddenly became quite interested in questions of life and death and what happens after we die.

Lewis agreed to the offer, and he soon began commuting from his home in Oxford to London to record the talks he had written. The broadcast talks went out to the entire country. They were incredibly popular, and soon Lewis became the most recognized voice in the country after Winston Churchill. What began as a

short series of fifteen-minute talks soon stretched to four different series, aired from 1941 to 1944. While each series of talks was
originally published independently, they were later published as
the compilation we know as *Mere Christianity*.

But these broadcast talks were far from all Lewis was doing
at the start of the 1940s. In addition to his teaching and lectures
at Oxford, traveling to speak to men in the Royal Air Force about
Christianity, and recording talks at the BBC in London, Lewis also
found time to write *The Screwtape Letters*. Originally published in
The Guardian—not the London newspaper, but an Anglican peri-
odical—Lewis said the idea for this imaginary correspondence
between an elder demon and his young apprentice came to him
one Sunday morning as he was leaving church. Interestingly,
Lewis wrote in a letter that the night before he had been listening
to Hitler on the radio. Noting Hitler's impressive rhetorical prowess, Lewis said if one was not careful, he could quite quickly begin
thinking what he knew to be evil as good, and what he knew to
be good as evil. This sort of upside-down perspective is, of course,
precisely what we find in *The Screwtape Letters*' treatment of sin.
Though it was Lewis's least-favorite book to write, *The Screwtape
Letters* was an impressive commercial success, republished eight
times in its first year alone.

It was also at this time, during World War II, that Lewis
preached his famous sermon "The Weight of Glory" at the
University Church of St. Mary the Virgin in Oxford. This sermon
contains many well-known Lewis quotations, including his suggestion that "It would seem that Our Lord finds our desires not too
strong, but too weak. … We are far too easily pleased." Lewis's gardener, Fred Paxford, was in the audience the day Lewis delivered

"The Weight of Glory"; upon hearing Lewis preach, Paxford suggested that Lewis missed his calling—to be a preacher.

WRITTEN CORRESPONDENCE

Following the success of his BBC broadcast talks and *The Screwtape Letters*, C. S. Lewis became well known not only in England but also in the United States as a Christian apologist. Lewis's face even graced the cover of *Time* magazine on September 8, 1947. In addition to all this writing—likely in response to all this writing—Lewis also was replying to an overwhelming number of letters from those who had heard his BBC radio broadcast talks or who were reading his books.

Lewis would spend, on average, two hours each day replying to letters. He believed it was his duty—that anyone who took the time to write him deserved to receive a letter in response. Even more impressive, Lewis's letters weren't often brief generic replies, but long, thoughtful responses. If you get a chance, do take the time to check out the three-volume set of Lewis's letters. Many readers are surprised to find how incredibly rich Lewis's letters are; they are an oft-overlooked peek at Lewis's brilliant gift of writing.

Another interesting fact is that all of Lewis's writing, from his books to his letters, was done by hand. C. S. Lewis never used a typewriter, as he said it's important for writers to think about the cadence of their written words, and the typewriter's noise interferes. He also said that taking time to pause and think about what he was writing—which he was forced to do with a dip pen—helped his creativity.

Many of those who wrote to Lewis would become highly personal in their writing—particularly his American correspondents. This caught Lewis off guard, but he did his best to respond thoughtfully. Reading and replying to such candid notes gave Lewis deep insights into the human condition, in all its multifaceted forms, in a way he would not have otherwise had access to as an Oxford don.

Lewis's familiarity with the diversity of humanity is perhaps most clear in *The Great Divorce* (1946). In this imaginative account of a group of tourists from purgatory, Lewis poignantly illustrates lifelike characters facing very real struggles. Through these characters, Lewis describes what he believed were self-inflicted roadblocks preventing us from accepting the Lord's gift of grace, rather than God actively preventing us from this gift.

In 1947, Lewis's *Miracles: A Preliminary Study* was published. In this work, Lewis attempts to respond to the modern understanding of the world as a closed system, an ideology that rejects at the outset any suggestion of the miraculous. He goes on to make a case for the historical validity of the miracles found in the Old and New Testaments. However, a debate about one of Lewis's arguments from the book, which took place at the Oxford Socratic Club, has received even more attention than Lewis's work in the book itself. It has been said that, at the February 2, 1948, meeting of the Socratic Club, Elizabeth Anscombe presented a paper that some say embarrassed C. S. Lewis by debunking his argument for Christianity. Like most myths, there are hints of truth in this story, but mostly it is false. The truth is that Ms. Anscombe's paper, which critiqued the third chapter of *Miracles*, wherein Lewis argued that the naturalist position was self-refuting, caused Lewis to make revisions to this chapter in future editions of the book. However, not only was Ms. Anscombe not out to disprove Christianity (she was herself a practicing Roman Catholic), but her critiques were specifically of Lewis's setup for a very particular argument. Of course, that story is much less exciting than the myth that the great Christian apologist C. S. Lewis was embarrassed in a fierce debate and no longer able to defend his faith!

FOR REFLECTION

1 After hearing C. S. Lewis preach his sermon "The Weight of Glory," Lewis's gardener, Fred Paxford, suggested Lewis should have been a preacher. Do you think he was right? How might Lewis's impact on global Christianity have been different had he not been an academic, but a minister?

2 Even with an incredibly busy schedule of teaching his own students, writing and delivering lectures, writing his own books, and giving visiting lectures, C. S. Lewis still regularly took time to write in response to everyone who sought his counsel because he believed it was his duty. What can we learn from his example?

NARNIA, CAMBRIDGE, AND JOY

A MARKED CHANGE IN LEWIS'S WRITING

Perhaps none of Lewis's works are as well-known as his *Chronicles of Narnia* series. The Chronicles consist of seven books, written from 1949 to 1954, which display Lewis's powerful imagination at work. Captivating children young and old alike for generations, the Chronicles of Narnia have now sold more than 100 million copies and have been published in nearly 50 different languages!

The power of the Narnia stories, as has been noted by former Archbishop of Canterbury Rowan Williams, is that they allow us to feel what Christianity means from the inside. As Alister McGrath notes in his biography of Lewis: "*Mere Christianity* allows us to understand Christian ideas; the Narnia stories allow us to step inside and *experience* the Christian story."[4]

While much could be said about the Chronicles, we will touch on just one question here: Why did Lewis write the Chronicles? At the time, many people were shocked that the world's most well-known Christian apologist had begun writing imaginative children's literature. Lewis was well aware of this, even before the books were released.

In light of such a surprising turn in his writing, some people have suggested, and actually still suggest today, that Lewis began writing this series as a retreat from the academic world of apologetics and as a way to infiltrate the minds of the youth, persuading them to Christianity without their knowing it (see, for example, A. N. Wilson's biography of C. S. Lewis, as well as Philip Pullman's His Dark Materials books).

Lewis heard this story himself, and he rejected it outright. Rather than strategizing how he might convert the hearts and minds of children through imaginative stories, Lewis argued that he was simply writing about images—of a faun, a queen, a lion—that came to him, and which he could not shake (for his full description, see "Sometimes Fairy Stories May Say Best What's to be Said"). In this way, Lewis was actually quite humble about his most popular writing—suggesting it wasn't even his idea, but something given to him, an image from somewhere beyond himself.

FROM BACHELOR TO HUSBAND AND FATHER: LEWIS'S LIFE IN THE 1950s

In the early 1950s, at the very time that his most famous Narnia Chronicles were being published, Lewis experienced significant changes in his personal life, starting with the death of the woman with whom he had been living since he was a student at Oxford.

After Maureen Moore got married and moved out of the Kilns in 1939, Mrs. Moore continued to live at the Kilns with Lewis and his brother Warnie until she was moved to an elderly care facility in North Oxford in 1950. Lewis visited Mrs. Moore there every day until she passed away in 1951.

After Mrs. Moore's passing, it was just Lewis and his brother Warnie living at the Kilns. The house quickly began to look like a bachelor pad. For starters, there were books everywhere—stacked from floor to ceiling in most rooms, down the hallways, and even up the spiral staircase. One literary critic described Lewis as the most well read man in England during his life; his house suggested this might very well be true.

Then, there were the Lewis brothers' more bizarre habits. Both brothers were heavy smokers; while that wasn't unusual at the time, it was enough to turn the walls and ceilings in their home yellow. After they had finished smoking their pipes, it's said that Lewis and Warnie would often dump the ash on the rug in the middle of the front room and then stomp it in with their shoes. They used to like to joke that this helped to preserve the carpets, as it kept the moths away. Truth be told, it actually kept some of their friends away: after seeing the state of the house at this time, J. R. R. Tolkien was no longer allowed to come over, as his wife was sure he would get sick just from being there! It was around this time that Lewis's friends affectionately nicknamed the Kilns the "dung heap."

JOY DAVIDMAN

With their house in this condition, the Lewis brothers were visited for the first time by Joy Davidman, a Jewish New Yorker who had been writing Lewis for several years. A former atheist and member of the Communist Party, Joy had converted to Christianity—and, according to Joy, Lewis's writings were instrumental in her conversion. She continued reading Lewis's writing even after her conversion, his voice becoming a sort of spiritual guide.

Some time after her conversion, Joy began writing Lewis—as so many others did—and Lewis would reply with thoughtful responses—as he so often did. But Lewis and Joy had much in common, more than most who wrote Lewis. For one, Joy was brilliant. A child prodigy with an IQ of more than 150, Joy graduated from high school at fourteen and went on to attend university in New York at age fifteen. It's said that she was one of the few people—men or women—who could keep up with Lewis in a debate.

Joy earned her MA in literature from Columbia: not only was she brilliant, but she shared Lewis's appreciation for literature. Before converting to Christianity, Joy had served as the editor of the national Communist magazine, worked as a freelance writer, and had published both prose and poetry. It's little surprise Lewis and Joy got along so well so quickly.

After writing back and forth for a few years, Joy visited the Lewis brothers in Oxford in 1952. That December, Joy spent a two-week holiday with Lewis and Warnie at the Kilns. The following year, Joy returned to England with her two sons: David, the older, and Douglas, the younger. The family first took a flat in London and later moved to Oxford, about a mile from Lewis's home.

Not long after moving to Oxford, the British government found out about Joy's former ties to the Communist Party (not a popular affiliation in the 1950s) and threatened her with extradition. Realizing how stressful this would be on her young family after only recently moving from the United States to England, Joy and Lewis, now good friends, entered into a civil union to ensure Joy could remain living in England with her two sons. This was no romantic engagement that took place in Oxford's Registry Office on April 23, 1956, but merely one friend helping another.

The following October (1956), Joy was diagnosed with bone cancer and sent to the hospital. At this point, Lewis and Joy realized they were actually more fond of one another than they had previously realized, and a wedding ceremony was performed on what they thought might be Joy's deathbed. The Reverend Peter Bide both performed the marriage ceremony in the hospital in Oxford on March 21, 1957, and also laid hands on Joy and prayed for her recovery.

The following month, Joy was able to move into the Kilns with her husband and her two boys. By December, she was able to walk again, and by June 1958, Joy's cancer was in remission. Joy and Lewis enjoyed three wonderful years of marriage—even vacationing in Greece—before her cancer finally returned. She passed away in July 1960.

Just one month after Joy's death, Lewis wrote *A Grief Observed*, a painfully honest account of his struggles with grief. In fact, Lewis wrestled so candidly with his grief in the book that he actually used a pseudonym when it was first published.

LEWIS'S FINAL YEARS

One thing many people don't realize is that C. S. Lewis actually spent most of the final decade of his teaching career at the University of Cambridge, not Oxford. Lewis gave his final Oxford tutorial at the end of 1954 and took up his new post at Cambridge at the start of 1955, assuming a chair position created specifically with him in mind.

In 1961, Lewis was diagnosed with an enlarged prostate gland. Unfortunately, the doctors were unable to operate, as it was simply too dangerous, and by October of that year Lewis had become too ill to teach any longer. He continued to receive honorary doctorates (from the University of Dijon and the University of Lyon) and speaking requests, but his work at that point was limited to writing from home.

C. S. Lewis passed away in his home, shortly after taking afternoon tea, on November 22, 1963—the same day as John F. Kennedy's assassination and the death of Aldous Huxley, author of *Brave New World*.

News of President Kennedy's assassination was so massive that it largely overshadowed news of Lewis's death. Even some of Lewis's own friends didn't know of his death until after his funeral. As a result, the funeral was poorly attended. Lewis was buried at Holy Trinity Church, a small Anglican church not far from his home, where he had attended since the 1930s. A line from Shakespeare's *King Lear* is carved on his gravestone; it reads, "Men must endure their going hence." It is the same line that was found on a Shakespearean calendar hanging on the wall of his parents' bedroom the day Lewis's mother passed away, when Lewis was just a young boy, and which Albert Lewis preserved for the rest of his life.

FOR REFLECTION

1 Though the Chronicles of Narnia are Lewis's most well-known works, their appearance at the start of the 1950s would have surprised many of Lewis's readers. In what ways did his new literary direction build on—rather than retreat from, as some said—his efforts to articulate the Christian faith?

2   C. S. Lewis was nearly 60 years old when he married Joy Davidman. This surprising love story has taken many shapes in both stage and film adaptations. What are some of the ways their story has been misconstrued? What can we learn from their story?

3   In the final year of his life, C. S. Lewis wrote *Letters to Malcolm: Chiefly on Prayer*, an attempt to help others with the some-times-difficult business of private prayer. In this book, we see Lewis using his sharp intellect, literary prowess, and his own experience as a Christian as a means to help others with their own faith—right up until the end of his life. This is not a path Lewis could have predicted for his life, particularly during his years as an atheist. How does this ending to Lewis's life encourage you in your own life and faith or those of your loved ones?

THE GREAT DIVORCE

DID YOU KNOW?

C. S. Lewis wrote himself into several of his books as a character in the story. In addition to playing the central character in *The Great Divorce*, Lewis also plays a cameo role in his science fiction series, the Space Trilogy.

Lewis also wrote one of his favorite writers into *The Great Divorce*: George MacDonald (1824–1905), a Scottish author and Christian minister.

Lewis originally proposed the title *Who Goes Home?* for the book.

While C. S. Lewis didn't finish writing *The Great Divorce* until 1944, his brother Warnie noted Lewis's idea for this book in his diary in 1933, making it one of Lewis's first recorded book ideas after his own Christian conversion.

Lewis credits Jeremy Taylor, a seventeenth-century Anglican, for giving him the idea of a holiday from hell (which he developed in *The Great Divorce*).

INTRODUCTION AND HEAVEN AS TOTAL REALITY

IN EPISODE 5, PROFESSOR ASH INTRODUCES US TO ONE OF C. S. Lewis's great fictional works, *The Great Divorce*. This is an imagined account of what it might be like for a group of tourists to travel on vacation to the outskirts of heaven. What might they find there? What might it be like? And, also, what affect would this experience have on them?

As the name implies, and as Professor Ash emphasizes, Lewis is here interested in the separation between heaven and hell. What is most interesting about this work, though, is not the idea of heaven and hell's separation, but *why* they're separated. What could possibly keep back any soul fortunate enough to travel from hell to heaven from entering into the pearly gates of God's presence? (Do remember that Lewis himself insists, in the beginning of the book, that we take this scenario as imaginative, not as an orthodox description of the afterlife!) That answer is as multifaceted as the human condition—which Lewis knew quite well, thanks to his correspondence with the many people who wrote him. And it is here, in *The Great Divorce*, that C. S. Lewis painfully acutely portrays the ways in which we ourselves refuse to accept God's gift of grace in our lives—choosing, instead, the hellish reality of separation from God.

HEAVEN IS REAL; HELL IS A NO-THING

As Professor Ash notes, one of the first observations made by those traveling from hell to the outskirts of heaven is that they are virtually invisible. At the same time, their newfound surroundings are so densely real that even the stem of a daisy is too strong to break by hand, and the blades of grass are like spikes, piercing to walk on.

What is Lewis getting at with these descriptions of the hellish characters and their new, heavenly surroundings? Likely, he has at least two points in mind. First, note that the Christian conception of good and evil, heaven and hell, is not that these are equal and opposing parties. Good is supreme; evil is parasitic and subservient. Likewise, sin is not a power on par with righteousness, attempting to overthrow God's kingdom, but is instead no-thing. To live into sin is to remove oneself further and further away from God, not into a realm competing with God, but away from our very life source. In this way, Lewis is quite right to depict those from hell as waif-like or nearly invisible and the elements and people of heaven as densely substantive and real—real in the fullest sense. Christianity supports no form of dualism, but always and only the invitation to live into the kind of life that is properly described as life, unlike some forms of life that are more properly described as death. Or, as Jesus put it: "The thief comes only to steal and kill and destroy. I came that they may have life and have it abundantly" (John 10:10).

Second, Lewis also shows that the benefits of heaven are not the sort of benefits that someone in hell would be interested in, even if they could be abstracted from heaven. Often heaven is conceived of as a bail—goods or rewards that those who have not lived with any interest in God or God's desire for their life might somehow receive anyway. But Lewis illustrates that heaven will not satisfy the tastes of such people because their tastes have not been properly prepared for heaven—it is too substantial, too real, too weighty for their palettes. Far from being a treasure chest of rewards they might receive by God's generous grace, heaven would not fit their interests. Even if they could come face to face with such heavenly treasures, Lewis suggests, they would not receive them as treasure; they would be too wrapped up in the hellish reality from which they had come. Their senses have been distorted, preventing them from seeing the gift staring them right in the face. This experience, then, is not to be understood as a terrible injustice to those in hell, but a depressing, nightmarish depiction of a failure to rightly perceive good as good and evil as evil.

FOR REFLECTION

1   It has been suggested that *The Great Divorce* supports Universalism, the idea that, in the end, all will be saved. Why might this be a false interpretation of Lewis's intended meaning?

2 How might Lewis's depiction of the painful distinction between those from heaven and the reality of heaven be helpful in responding to those who seek the benefits of heaven without any regard for God or God's desire for right human living?

HEAVEN'S TOURISTS

O NE OF THE MOST POWERFUL ASPECTS OF *THE GREAT DIVORCE* is its poignant depiction of the human visitors from hell to heaven and what keeps them from accepting the opportunity to remain in heaven. Professor Ash introduces a variety of these hellish characters' conversations with heavenly characters; we will consider them in closer detail here.

THE POET: THE PERPETUAL VICTIM

Taking a seat beside Lewis on the bus bound for heaven is a "tousle-haired" young man called the Poet whose life had been plagued by what he suggested was "ill luck." While on their ride, the young Poet explains to Lewis of all the injustices he's faced, his talents being completely overlooked by both his parents and his many schools. Soon, the Poet comes to the conclusion that he's not merely a victim of countless, random injustices, but that all of these wrongs are the inevitable result of the economic system. This realization leads him to Communism. When a young girl's love failed him too, the Poet explains, he threw himself under a train.

Unlike the other passengers on their heaven-bound bus, the Poet is certain that he is going to stay on in the heavenly realm, where his exceptional talents will finally receive due recognition and appreciation. Like so many, the Poet believes that the full sum of his misfortunes have been a terrible oversight of his exceptional talent and superiority, which unfortunately leaves him unable to recognize the grace offered by heaven.

THE INTELLIGENT MAN: ECONOMIC SALVATION

Lewis soon finds himself seated beside another passenger on the heaven-bound bus: the "Intelligent Man." The trouble with those in hell, the Intelligent Man explains, is that they have no needs. In hell, you get whatever you want (though never of very good quality) simply by imagining it. His self-appointed job, then, is to travel to heaven and return with some real things: some viable goods or commodities. The so-called Intelligent Man isn't so sure heaven is the kind of place for him, but he believes it has something to offer those in hell: commodities to sell and purchase.

As Professor Ash notes, the Intelligent Man can be seen as a model of what might be called "economic salvation." He is intelligent enough to note that there is a problem with those in hell, but he is not quite intelligent enough to see that what is needed is far more than commodities to buy and sell. While he dreams of becoming a profitable entrepreneur, he misses the real gifts heaven has to offer those separated from its beauty and truth.

THE BIG MAN: SALVATION BY WORKS

One of the earliest characters Lewis comes across in his imaginative journey from hell to heaven is the "Big Man," or "Big Ghost."

Something of a bully, the Big Man is overly confident in himself (a pattern among these tourists) and his own efforts. Though, self-admittedly, he was not a religious man, the Big Man notes proudly that he had always done his best to be decent to everyone. Far from a gift freely given by God, heaven is a right that the Big Man thinks he deserves.

Professor Ash describes the Big Man as a model of salvation-by-works: he believes he deserves salvation because of his good works, even though he shows little to no interest in heaven other than as something to which he has a right. Indeed, the Big Man can often be found arguing for his rights. What he fails to realize, however, even after arriving in heaven, is that so long as he insists on his "rights," he will miss all heaven has to offer—which is much, much more than he can comprehend from his limited perspective.

THE APOSTATE CLERGYMAN: INTELLECTUAL SALVATION

As Professor Ash notes, it seems one of Lewis's favorite characters in *The Great Divorce* is the "Apostate Clergyman" in Chapter 5—perhaps, Professor Ash suggests, because Lewis had met one or two during his own time. In the book, the character Lewis comes across the Clergyman, a waif-like ghost who had been a passenger on the bus, in conversation with an old friend from earth named Dick, another clergyman, who is now abiding in heaven and giving off a brilliant white light. One of the first comments the Clergyman makes to his heavenly friend, Dick, is a suggestion that, surely, his views have broadened out since they last spoke, at the end of Dick's life: "Why, my dear boy, you were coming to believe in a literal Heaven and Hell!"

As the conversation continues, Dick reveals to the Clergyman that he has, indeed, been in hell as an apostate—though if he were to stay on in heaven it would be called purgatory. As becomes apparent, the issue for the apostate clergyman is intellectual salvation: he believes his own intellectual efforts and accomplishments make him deserving of heaven. Far from giving the apostate clergyman a pat on the back for what he considers intellectual bravery, Dick merely chalks this up to contemporary ideas and a desire to sell books.

With this, Dick encourages his apostate clergyman friend to repent and believe: "You have seen Hell: you are in sight of Heaven. Will you, even now, repent and believe?" But rather than accept the opportunity to repent and accept the gift of divine grace, the apostate clergyman insists that he must be getting back, as he has to present an important theological paper on the topic of how Christ would have outgrown many of his own ideas if his life not been cut short and his thought had had time to develop fully. And so, even with the offer on the table, the ghost Clergyman turns down the opportunity to see God face to face. In the end, his intellectual endeavors are a greater god to the Apostate Clergyman than is the true God.

THE VAIN WOMAN: IMAGE SALVATION

In Chapter 8, Lewis comes across a female ghost who is trying to hide herself from the spirits, ashamed by her waif-like appearance in their presence. Though the woman is dressed in some sort of fine clothing, her appearance is horrifying in the heavenly light. One heavenly spirit, unaffected by her appearance, tries to encourage her to let him take her to the heavenly mountains.

Unfortunately, she refuses. Even as the heavenly spirit insists that appearances no longer matter here, her shame regarding her appearance is too much for her to bear; she cannot allow herself to be seen as she is.

Unlike other visitors from hell, this woman's obstacle to accepting the divine gift before her is not intellect nor achievement, but appearance. The spirit pleads with the woman to turn her gaze away from herself—but with her gaze so transfixed by her looks, she cannot accept the offer of heaven even as it stands before her with hand outstretched.

FOR REFLECTION

1 For the characters we've discussed so far, everything from one's own efforts and looks to one's intellectual accomplishments have been imaginatively presented as obstacles to accepting God's free gift of grace. Which of these obstacles do you find yourself relating to more, either in conversations you've had with others or, more personally, from your own experience?

2 How does Lewis's characterization of these obstacles to accepting God's gift of grace help us communicate the gospel in a helpful way?

SECTION THREE

LEWIS MEETS HIS MENTOR

WEATHER-BEATEN SCOTCHMAN: GEORGE MACDONALD

Following his encounter with the vain woman in Chapter 8, Lewis meets the Scottish writer George MacDonald, a man whose writing influenced C. S. Lewis's work and thought. MacDonald's role as literary mentor to Lewis in real life is reflected imaginatively in their heavenly dialogue in *The Great Divorce*, as Lewis's character pelts the tall, radiant, and bearded Scotchman with question after question.

IS JUDGMENT FINAL? RETROSPECTIVE CHOICES

One of the first questions Lewis asks concerns judgment, and whether it is final: is there really a way out of hell into heaven? MacDonald's response is that, for those who choose to stay on in heaven, their time in the grey town only ever would have been purgatory, and their time in heaven will have been as though they had always been in heaven. By contrast, for those who choose to return, it is, indeed, hell. The whole matter, then, comes down to choice. Once the choice is made, the implications of that choice work backward. "And that is why," MacDonald's heavenly character explains, "at the end of all things, when the sun rises here and the twilight turns to blackness down there, the Blessed will say 'We have never lived anywhere except in Heaven,' and the Lost, 'We were always in Hell.' And both will speak truly."

The ideas of time and choice can be confusing, as MacDonald's character notes in Chapter 9. However, it is important to note here that Lewis seems less interested in emphasizing the importance of the *timing* of our choice, but more the choice itself. It would be tempting to enter into lengthy debates about whether or not such choices must be made on this side of death or not, but, at least for Lewis, what matters is that people choose rightly and trust that the implications of their choice, having been made, will work themselves out—for better or for immeasurably worse.

HOW COULD ANY CHOOSE HELL?

Perplexed by the idea that any would *choose* not to enter into heaven, Lewis asks MacDonald about the lost ones who choose hell. The response given by Lewis's mentor is that, like a spoiled child who will pass up a meal in order to avoid apologizing, there are those who refuse to surrender and accept the gift of grace out of a desire to keep something back—whether it be one's vanity, feelings of victimization, pride, or countless other obstacles to God. "There is always something they prefer to joy," MacDonald explains in Chapter 9.

Such an explanation is a depressing portrait, to be sure, and yet it feels true to experience. As MacDonald's character puts it:

"There are only two kinds of people in the end: those who say to God, 'Thy will be done', and those to whom God says, in the end, '*Thy* will be done.'" The choice is always on the side of the individual person, either to accept God's free gift of grace, or to hold out for one's own individual autonomy, even in great misery. No one is lost who has not freely chosen it, Lewis insists. And, likewise, if anyone so chooses, their final and fullest existence will be one of unending, genuine joy in God's presence.

FOR REFLECTION

1 Lewis's explanation of our choices working retroactively, so that those who choose heaven will have always been in heaven, and those who choose their separation from God will have always been lost, can be confusing. What matters to Lewis is not so much the relation between choice and timing, but an insistence on choice. How might you describe this to someone who has not read *The Great Divorce*?

2 As noted above, Lewis (through the character of MacDonald) says that, in the end, there are only two types of people. In this way, Lewis puts the weight of one's choice of either heaven or hell on the individual, rather than God. What Bible passages come to mind to support this view? Do any come to mind that contradict this view?

SEVERAL ADDITIONAL CHARACTERS

FOLLOWING HIS CONVERSATION WITH HIS MENTOR, LEWIS watches as several more characters on holiday from hell encounter heavenly beings and face what are very real challenges to their accepting the opportunity to stay on. We will have a closer look at several now.

THE MARRIED WOMAN: DESIRES OTHERS TO CONTROL

One of the characters Lewis encounters, in Chapter 10, is a woman who was married to a man named Walter, whom she took great pleasure in setting straight, for what, on the surface, was for his benefit. However, while her description of their relationship comes off as selfless benevolence toward her ill-witted husband, it quickly becomes clear that the woman's efforts were all really for her own sake, and her time apart from him has become intolerable as a result: she needs someone to control.

While such a depiction might seem so great an exaggeration that it is too comical to be helpful, there's a sense in which Lewis is right to point out that, for some, our controlling nature can overpower any desire for happiness or joy in God's intended sense for our life. For some of us, our desires have become so narrowly focused that we simply cannot imagine the heavenly reality toward which God is calling us. Ultimately, the woman in question cannot fathom a heaven in which she doesn't have her husband, Robert, to change. And, as a result, she cannot fathom heaven at all.

MICHAEL'S MOTHER:
HEAVEN AS BELOVED REUNION

The next episode, in Chapter 11, is one that Lewis himself describes as among the hardest encounters he witnesses during this journey. The meeting in question involves an encounter between a woman ghost and a spirit who was her brother on earth. Their conversation soon turns to the woman's son, Michael, whom she desperately wants to see. The difficult lesson this woman soon faces is that, before she can see Michael, she must learn to want "Something Else" than her son.

What soon becomes clear is that, for the woman, any talk of religion, heaven, or God is only a means to her son. What the ghost fails to realize, of course—like so many others we've already discussed—is that God must be sought first and foremost, as the ultimate and true end, not as a means to some other end.

This scene brings to mind a misconception many people hold of heaven: as some sort of family reunion on the celestial shores. In this conception of eternity, heaven is no more than a gathering of loved ones in the sky. But is that an appropriate picture of heaven? Is that a biblical conception of eternity? Lewis here appears to dispel any such suggestion: heaven is no mere celestial reunion of loved ones. It is, before anything else, the opportunity to be in the full presence of God, which is our true satisfaction.

But the female ghost in this scene is not satisfied with this explanation. It appears to her that her spirit-brother has not understood—indeed, that he cannot understand her motherly love, "the highest and holiest feeling in human nature."

The correction that comes is twofold. First, what the mother fails to see is that her role as mother is superseded by her role as God's creature, which must come first. The only reason she is a mother is because she is God's first. Further, she is told that so long as she seeks to be satisfied by her son, she will never be fully satisfied. She can only be made whole when she comes to God. Were she to receive her son as she is, she would only attempt to bring him back to hell with her, which would not only leave her unsatisfied but would mean her son's harm as well.

Ultimately, what the ghost needs to hear—and seems unable to receive—is that her love for Michael isn't *real* love. Her love for her son is, in a way, self-love. It is a desire to have him for herself—which is not true love, even if she refers to it as the highest form of love. In fact, her love for her son will only be what it ought to be when it is first seeking God. So long as her love is first directed at anything other than God, it will turn the object of its affection into an idol, and it will ultimately turn sour, as the spirit warns her.

This is, of course, completely counterintuitive to cultural portrayals of love, which tempt us not only to place utmost importance in familial relationships, but also to make romantic relationships our ultimate pursuit. But such love, Lewis warns, will not only never satisfy us as we're led to believe it will; it will also turn us away from that which will truly satisfy—namely, God—so long as it's pursued as an end in itself. The difficult lesson that this ghost, and so many others, fails to understand is that any loves in our life must be surrendered to God and subordinated to our love for God in order for them to be a source of joy and blessing and not an obstacle to our ultimate joy. As George MacDonald puts it to Lewis's character in Chapter 11 of *The Great Divorce*: "Love, as mortals understand the word, isn't enough. Every natural love will rise again and live forever in this country: but none will rise again until it has been buried."

THE YOUNG MAN WITH LIZARD: LUST AS OBSTACLE TO HEAVEN

One of the last characters Lewis meets on his heavenly tour is a young male ghost; on his shoulder sits a small, red lizard, which constantly whips its tail around and whispers into the ghost's ear. When Lewis first sees the ghost, he is moving toward the mountains. But after a whisper from the lizard on his shoulder, the ghost turns and makes his way back to the bus.

The ghost is then greeted by a spirit who is brighter than any of the other spirits that Lewis has seen—an angel. The angel offers to remove the lizard from the ghost's shoulder, as it is quite clearly getting in the way. While the young male ghost initially concedes, when he realizes that the angel's burning hands mean to kill the lizard, the ghost resists. Even after the angel insists that the only way to get rid of this lizard is to kill it, the young ghost finds excuse after excuse to avoid such a response: it's embarrassing, but just now it has gone to sleep. Surely it will be all right now. No need to bother with its death.

What Lewis is portraying here is a young man's love-hate relationship with lust. While he hates his struggle with lust—which he realizes are keeping him back from going further up and further in to the heavenly realm—he is not yet ready to part ways with this temptation. Such a portrait is reminiscent of St. Augustine's well-known prayer: "Lord, make me chaste (sexually pure)—but not yet."

When the angel moves in to kill the object of the ghost's temptation with lust, the ghost complains of being burned. He wonders if the lizard's death will also effect his own. The angel insists this is not the case, even though it is likely to hurt at first; however, the lizard cannot be killed without the ghost's permission. Finally after some reluctance, the permission is granted and the angel grasps the lizard. The result is shocking: the young ghost suddenly grows solid, bright, and of great strength—almost as large as the angel. What's more, the lizard is suddenly transformed into a great, white stallion with a golden mane and tail. The man leaps on the stallion and shoots off into the mountains like a star, both the ghost and the lizard transformed into heavenly creatures of angelic beauty.

The lesson from this scene, MacDonald explains, is that not even the lowliest aspects of human nature are beyond redemption. But, before they can enter heaven, they must face their death. Only that which has been submitted to God can be raised to new, eternal, full life.

FOR REFLECTION

1   How does Lewis's portrait of Michael's mother provide a correction to the view of heaven as merely a celestial reunion with loved ones?

2   It is not uncommon to hear that people cannot believe in a God who would allow someone's untimely death, which is precisely the argument made by Michael's mother as she mourns her separation from her son. While the death of a child is always difficult and worth our lament, how is her belief that "motherly love" is the highest form of love in need of correction?

3   In the scene of the young man with the lizard whispering in his ear, we find a powerful portrait of one of the deep lies of sin: if we lose a particular temptation, we will be losing a crucial piece of our identity. What does Lewis's depiction of the ghost turning solid and strong and the lizard transforming into a beautiful stallion teach us about such temptations?

A HOLIDAY TO HEAVEN
COMES TO AN END

B EFORE LEWIS CONCLUDES HIS TIME IN HEAVEN, LEWIS AND MacDonald discuss some of the most important objections to Christianity's depiction of heaven and hell. One such question posed to MacDonald is: How can anyone ever really be content in heaven if their loved ones are in hell? In an interesting turn of perspective, Lewis via MacDonald suggests that this question sounds merciful, but what it actually suggests is a demanding terror. If those who are in hell ultimately choose hell, and if they've been given the option of heaven, then why should those who have rightly chosen heaven be prevented from enjoying it to the fullest by those who have refused this gift? As MacDonald puts it, this amounts to no more than "the demand of the loveless and the self-imprisoned that they should be allowed to blackmail the universe: that till they consent to be happy (on their own terms) no one else shall taste joy."

Those in heaven will be fully satisfied, Lewis here insists, regardless of whether or not other souls persist in their refusal to enter into this joy. The latter shall not hold the former back from enjoying this free gift that God has offered to all.

Reflecting on Christ's descent into hell following his crucifixion, Lewis asks MacDonald if Christ will return again to hell, offering the opportunity for repentance. In what has become a common theme, MacDonald replies that the nature of eternity and time means that Christ's descent into hell made this offer a present reality for all those in hell.

HELL: A SPLINTER COMPARED TO HEAVEN

Before concluding their conversation, Lewis offers a powerful picture of the size of hell compared to heaven. Bending down to his knee, MacDonald plucks a blade of grass and points to a crack in the ground that is so small Lewis can barely see it. To Lewis's astonishment, MacDonald tells Lewis that this crack is how Lewis entered heaven, pointing to the miniature size of hell in contrast to the immensity of heaven. Here, as before, Lewis is interested in showing the qualitative difference between heaven and hell.

While he was making his bus-bound journey to heaven, Lewis looked out over the whole of hell and was taken aback by how vast it seemed, and how very far each soul seemed from the next. But now, with his heavenly perspective, Lewis sees rightly that hell is nothing in comparison to the immeasurable reality of heaven: "For a damned soul is nearly nothing: it is shrunk, shut up in itself," MacDonald explains. As Lewis explains throughout his writings, Christianity does not teach that good and evil are equal but opposing interests. Instead, the evil of hell is, indeed, a no-thing in comparison to the good of heaven.

FOR REFLECTION

1 In his conversation with MacDonald, C. S. Lewis's character in *The Great Divorce* asks how anyone could fully enjoy heaven if even one soul remains in hell. This is a common critique of Christianity's understanding of hell. How does MacDonald's explanation sit with you? Can you use it in response to such questions?

2 By having MacDonald's character point to the full breadth of hell with nothing more than a blade of grass, Lewis suggests that hell is nothing in comparison to the reality of heaven. Heaven is everlastingly greater than we can imagine, Lewis creatively and emphatically suggests here. How is this depiction of heaven and hell helpful when we think about the "little" choices in day-to-day life that shape us one way or the other?

3 In *The Great Divorce*, Lewis uses imaginative portraits of various souls to show that obstacles of all different sorts prevent us from accepting God's free gift of grace and eternal salvation. What obstacles in this story resonated with you?

EPISODE SIX

NARNIA, PART I

DID YOU KNOW?

C. S. Lewis was often asked the inspiration for his Narnia books. His response? A mental picture he could not shake of a faun carrying an umbrella and some packages through a snowy forest.

The original illustrations for Lewis's Narnia chronicles were created by Pauline Baynes (1922–2008), whose illustrations appeared in more than 100 books. She was referred to Lewis by his good friend J. R. R. Tolkien, as she had recently created illustrations for Tolkien's novella *Farmer Giles of Ham*.

Though a dear friend to C. S. Lewis, J. R. R. Tolkien was not fond of Lewis's Narnia series—taking issue, for example, with inconsistencies among the mythological figures, such as Father Christmas showing up in Narnia alongside nymphs, fauns, and talking animals.

During World War II, with the looming threat of air raids on London, children were evacuated from the city and sent to the homes of country residents. In 1939, three young schoolgirls were sent to live in safety at the country home, the Kilns, of a professor—not unlike the beginning of *The Lion, the Witch and the Wardrobe*.

Lewis dedicated *The Lion, the Witch and the Wardrobe* to Lucy, who was Lewis's goddaughter and the daughter of Owen Barfield, one of Lewis's closest friends. She was 14 years old when the book was written.

Lewis scholar Dr. Michael Ward has suggested that medieval cosmology offers a symbolic, unifying coherence for the Chronicles of Narnia. He expounds on this theory in great detail in his twin books *Planet Narnia* (2007) and *The Narnia Code* (2010), showing that Lewis based each of the seven Narnia books on a different planet. *Prince Caspian*, for example, is inspired by the medieval symbolism of Mars. As a professor of English literature who studied and wrote extensively on English literature in the medieval period, C. S. Lewis would have been deeply familiar with medieval cosmology.

The Chronicles of Narnia is one of the bestselling book series of all times, crossing many cultural barriers. At the time of this writing, the series had been translated into nearly 50 languages.

READING ORDER

THE CHRONICLES OF NARNIA ARE MADE UP OF SEVEN BOOKS, published between 1950 and 1956. The first book published in the series was *The Lion, the Witch and the Wardrobe* (1950). However, there is a book in the series that takes place earlier chronologically: *The Magician's Nephew* (1955). Even though it was published second to last in the Narnia series, the events in *The Magician's Nephew* take place before all the others, which has resulted in a fair amount of controversy among Narnia enthusiasts regarding the order in which the Narnia series should be read.

Some insist that the Narnia series should be read according to the order in which C. S. Lewis originally wrote the books—which means saving *The Magician's Nephew* for last, since Lewis actually finished writing *The Last Battle* before *The Magician's Nephew*. However, there are others who say that since the events in *The Magician's Nephew* occur prior to the events in the other Narnia books, it should be read first. In addition, the events in *The Horse and His Boy* (1954) don't follow the publication order chronologically. Should it, then, be read in a different order? Perhaps it is worth asking what the author thought about the proper reading order?

Publication Order	Chronological Order
The Lion, the Witch and the Wardrobe (1950)	The Magician's Nephew
Prince Caspian (1951)	The Lion, the Witch and the Wardrobe
The Voyage of the Dawn Treader (1952)	The Horse and His Boy
The Silver Chair (1953)	Prince Caspian
The Horse and His Boy (1954)	The Voyage of the Dawn Treader
The Magician's Nephew (1955)	The Silver Chair
The Last Battle (1956)	The Last Battle

In a letter dated April 21, 1957, Lewis suggested that perhaps it would be easiest if the books were read in chronological order— that is, in the order in which the events unfold in Narnia. According to this approach, *The Magician's Nephew* should then be read first, before any other book in the Narnia series. However, he also noted in the same letter that "perhaps it does not matter very much in which order anyone reads them."[1] It is worth noting that, when he wrote *The Lion, the Witch and the Wardrobe*, Lewis did not know that he would be writing six more books in the Narnia series. This could play a role in why Lewis appears ambivalent about the reading order.

While publishers have now moved *The Magician's Nephew* to the first book in the series, citing Lewis's above letter as reason for this decision, there is good reason to read the books in the order in which they were published. One reason to follow the publication order, rather than the internal chronological order, is that *The Magician's Nephew* includes much knowledge that it assumes readers already know—which, of course, would not be known by readers who pick it up first in the series. For example, the word "Narnia" is used in the very first paragraph of *The Magician's Nephew*; those who have not already read *The Lion, the Witch and the Wardrobe* wouldn't already be familiar with the place. Further, *The Magician's Nephew* concludes with an explanation of the famed wardrobe's origins, which, again, would not be familiar to readers who have not already experienced *The Lion, the Witch and the Wardrobe*. Lastly, reading *The Magician's Nephew* according to its published order, and not before the rest of the books, gives it a powerful "flashback" effect, which illuminates the other books in the series in a way it would not do so if read first. These reasons and others might suggest reading the Narnia books according to their published order.

BACKGROUND TO THE CHRONICLES OF NARNIA

IN THIS VIDEO, PROFESSOR ASH INTRODUCES US TO ARGUABLY C. S. Lewis's most well-known works: The Chronicles of Narnia. The Chronicles consist of seven books, written from 1949 to 1954, which have captivated readers young and old alike for generations. The Chronicles of Narnia have been published in nearly 50 different languages and have sold more than 100 million copies.

In this first of two episodes on the Narnia Chronicles, Professor Ash will introduce us to several important themes in these books, as well as a close look at two in particular: *The Magician's Nephew* and *The Lion, the Witch and the Wardrobe*. But first, we will spend some time considering the background of these books and how they came to be.

WHY WRITE THE CHRONICLES?

Many today who are not at all familiar with C. S. Lewis or who might not even be Christian still appreciate the Narnia Chronicles. However, at the time of their writing, many were surprised that the world's most well-known Christian apologist had begun writing *children's* fiction. Lewis was well aware of this response.

Some have suggested that Lewis began writing children's literature as a retreat from the academic world and the great debates of Christian apologetics—in which he could no longer compete. It was suggested that these books were Lewis's intended way to propagate the Christian faith to the next generation.

Lewis heard of this idea even during his own day; he rejected it as a farce. When asked why he began writing the Narnia Chronicles, Lewis explains that he was simply writing about an image of a faun that he could not shake, which appeared to him as early as age 16.

There are, of course, hints of Lewis's real-life experiences in the books. One such example, at the start of *The Lion, the Witch and the Wardrobe*, is the children leaving London as it was being bombed in World War II and being sent off to a professor's home in the country. This very situation unfolded in Lewis's own life during World War II: on September 2, 1939, the first evacuated children were sent out of London during the Blitz to stay at Lewis's home in Oxford. Not only was this experience mirrored in Lewis's writing, but it also gave this middle-aged bachelor firsthand experience with children in a way he would not have otherwise had in his daily life as an Oxford don. After a brief start that year, Lewis waited an entire year before taking up writing *The Lion, the Witch and the Wardrobe* in earnest, the first book of the seven-book Narnia series.

ASLAN

According to Lewis, he began writing the Narnia Chronicles because of unshakable images. Once he began writing, however, he soon found an entire world unfolding. As Lewis once put it, as soon as Aslan the lion entered the stories, he was central to not only the first book's coming together, but all of the rest of the stories.

Professor Ash suggests that one way to read the Narnia Chronicles is to follow Aslan as he appears across all of the different books. It's worth noting, though, in light of the confusion among readers concerning the character of Aslan, that Aslan should not be read as a perfect representation of Jesus Christ as he appeared in our world. Instead, Lewis suggested that what he tried to do in Narnia was to suppose that there might be such a world and ask what it might be like if the Son of God appeared in *that* world for the purpose of its redemption. By reading these stories in this way, we find our own Christian faith illumined more brightly through the light of Narnia.

DIVISIONS: THE BIG THREE

Professor Tony Ash suggests that, among the seven books that make up the Chronicles of Narnia, we find what he refers to as "The Big Three": *The Magician's Nephew*; *The Lion, the Witch and the Wardrobe*; and *The Last Battle*. According to Professor Ash, what we find in these three books is an imaginative retelling of three core biblical stories: creation (*The Magician's Nephew*); death and resurrection (*The Lion, the Witch and the Wardrobe*); and the end times (*The Last Battle*). These are not the only biblical themes found in the Narnia Chronicles, but they can serve as a helpful way in to the Narnia stories.

For those familiar with the Genesis account of creation, reading *The Magician's Nephew* can offer a fresh perspective on the

Christian story of creation and evil's appearance in the formerly Edenic world. Likewise, the powerful picture of Aslan slain on the stone in *The Lion, the Witch and the Wardrobe* provides a fresh look at the poignancy of Christ's passion as recorded for us in the Gospels as well as the majesty of the resurrection.

Lewis noted other biblical themes in the Narnia books. For example, in *Prince Caspian* we read of the kind of corruption that befell ancient Israel's faith in the Old Testament on multiple occasions, as well as its restoration under the Lord's guiding hand. Likewise, we read of the calling and conversion of heathen in *The Horse and His Boy*. By reading the Narnia stories as more indirect retellings of the biblical narratives that can nevertheless lend a fresh perspective on the stories and themes of Scripture, the Narnia books can become illuminating devotionals even for adult readers—certainly much more than mere children's stories.

FOR REFLECTION

1 Even during his own day, C. S. Lewis was criticized for writing the Narnia Chronicles as a form of Christian propaganda for children. Why does this not fit with Lewis's own explanation of why he wrote the Narnia books?

2   C. S. Lewis defines allegory as the visual representation of an immaterial reality, such as the character of Cupid personifying love. Some have said that Aslan, and the Narnia Chronicles at large, should be read as allegory. Why would this be a mistake?

3   How might reading the Narnia Chronicles as a devotional be helpful for adult readers? Would this approach work for seasoned Christians as well as seekers?

THE MAGICIAN'S NEPHEW

READING ORDER

Even though it was published second to last in the Narnia series, *The Magician's Nephew* (1955) is set before all the others. In this way, as a prequel to the Narnia series, *The Magician's Nephew* illuminates the rest of the Narnia books with a rich background perspective. Because of the difference between its setting and its publication date in relation to the other Narnia books, quite some controversy has arisen regarding the order in the series which *The Magician's Nephew* should occupy. Professor Ash suggests that it should be read according to the order in which it was written (second to last in the series), not as the first book in the series.

SYNOPSIS & CHARACTERS

In *The Magician's Nephew*, C. S. Lewis tells the tale of Digory, a young boy living in London whose father is traveling in India and whose mother is deathly ill. Digory resides with his aunt and his uncle Andrew, a magician whose work leads to a journey that makes up the rest of the tale. Along with his neighbor, Polly, Digory magically travels to the world of Charn. Upon their arrival, the two children find that Charn is a world that has been destroyed by Jadis, an evil queen who has been put under a sleeping spell and who later becomes the White Witch of the Narnia series. Jadis is awakened by Digory falling to temptation, and when the two children try to escape Charn, Jadis follows them back to London, and, eventually, on to Narnia.

When they arrive in Narnia, the children are joined not only by Jadis, but also by Digory's uncle (Andrew), a cabby (Frank), and his cab-drawn horse (Strawberry). They also arrive in Narnia at a very important time: the event of creation. Here, the children witness Aslan breathing Narnia into being, including both nontalking animals as well as talking animals. The children travel by way of a winged horse (formerly Strawberry, but now named Fledge) to a secret garden where trees grow golden apples with magical healing powers that could, as Digory realizes, heal his mother. Though he has been told not to take the apples and eat them, he is tempted by Jadis to do just that. Ultimately, Digory resists the temptation, and Aslan provides him with an apple not only to heal his mother, but also to plant seeds that grow into a tree. This tree becomes the wardrobe that we see—along with a much older Digory, known as Professor Kirke—in *The Lion, the Witch and the Wardrobe*.

BIBLICAL THEMES

The Magician's Nephew includes several important biblical themes worth exploring, many of which center around the creation account in Scripture. As Professor Ash notes in the video, the biblical tale of creation is shown in a rich, creative way in *The Magician's*

Nephew: in Chapters 8 and 9 of the book, readers are granted a powerful picture of Aslan the lion breathing Narnia into being.

At first, Aslan sings a song that sets the formerly dark sky overhead ablaze with thousands upon thousands of stars. To some, such as Digory and Frank the Cabby, this song is described as the most beautiful noise, causing the cabby to exclaim that if he knew there were such a voice, he would have been a better man. For others, such as Uncle Andrew and Jadis the Witch, it is a deeply unsettling song, to which they respond in fear and anger.

Soon the sky opens up to reveal hills on the horizon and, before long, the sun itself, illuminating a valley of richly colored earth and a river flowing eastward. Finally, the eyes of the characters fall on Aslan himself, singing the entire scene into being, producing feelings of fear and flight in Uncle Andrew and Jadis. Creation continues to unfold as these two fight and argue, with the entire scene soon covered in green blades of grass, flowers of all varieties, and trees. Aslan's song continues, though changing at times, and the earth itself, now covered in shrubbery, swelled into humps that finally crumble, revealing animals of all sorts and varieties, all making such incredible noise that Aslan's voice becomes hard to hear. However, Aslan's voice, which has now spoken all of creation into being, produces in the human bystanders one of two reactions: either the desire to run and hug others, or the desire to fight.

Two important biblical themes that appear in *The Magician's Nephew*, which we will now consider, are covenant and temptation.

COVENANT

Following the creation of all of Narnia's animals, Aslan approaches the animals in pairs and touch their noses with his own. Out of all the deer, two deer are chosen; out of all the leopards, two chosen. Eventually, Aslan is surrounded by an enormous circle of animals who, after being touched by the great lion, "instantly left their own kinds and followed him." In contrast, those who were untouched went away.

Looking on at Aslan, the remaining animals begin to change. The small animals grow larger, while the larger animals grow smaller. With the humans still watching, Aslan opens his mouth and breathes on the animals present. A flash erupts across this entire scene, injuring no one, and Aslan speaks to the beasts, calling them to awake, to talk, to love, and to think.

At the start of Chapter 10, Aslan tells these chosen animals that the animals he has not chosen, the "Dumb Beasts," are to be treated with love. But, he warns them, the chosen animals are not to return to their former ways or else they will cease to be "Talking Beasts."

TEMPTATION

Toward the end of *The Magician's Nephew*, the children take an adventure on the now-winged Strawberry, who has received the new name Fledge, to a secret garden in the Western Wild. They are given the task of returning with a golden apple that has healing powers. As his mother is ill back home, Digory is tempted to do precisely that which he has been told not to do: to take one of the golden apples for himself. Indeed, when Digory enters the garden he finds that Jadis the Witch is already there, feasting on the forbidden fruit, and encouraging him to join her. Rather than return the fruit to Aslan, she encourages him to eat it himself, with the promise that he will never die, and that he and she can rule as king and queen.

With little effort, Digory brushes off the Witch's promise of eternal life, but it is her follow-up temptation that sticks deeper into his heart. "What about this mother of yours," she asks Digory. "Do you not see, Fool, that one bit of that apple would heal her?"

Digory is face-to-face with the thing he wants more than anything else—his mother's recovery—and is tempted to believe that he can have just that, if only he betrays Aslan. The Witch makes her temptation stronger and stronger, pulling on the young boy's emotions, asking how he or his father could ever forgive him for passing up the opportunity to save his mother.

Finally, Digory is able to see through the Witch's temptation and, jumping on Fledge beside Polly, flees the garden, returning to Narnia and giving Aslan the requested fruit, untouched.

With this, Digory is welcomed and received with a "well done" by Aslan. Later, Aslan explains that those who eat of the fruit ultimately resent the fruit's effects. Digory confesses his temptation to take the apple to his ill mother in hopes of curing her, and he asks Aslan if it actually would have healed her as the Witch promised. Aslan explains that although she would have been healed, it would have been a bitter healing; "you and she would have looked back and said it would have been better to die in that illness."

Much to Digory's surprise, Aslan then encourages him to pluck an apple from the tree—which, though it will not mean eternal life, will bring joy and healing to his ill mother. At this, Digory's entire world feels turned upside-down as he takes the fruit and returns home.

FOR REFLECTION

1   How does C. S. Lewis's portrait of the creation of Narnia in Chapters 8–9 of *The Magician's Nephew* compare to the creation account found in Genesis 1–2? How does his description of Narnia's creation illuminate Scripture's description of the creation of our world?

2   Though it is far from a perfect analogy, Aslan choice of some animals in Chapter 10 of *The Magician's Nephew* seems to parallel God's covenant with a particular people in the Old Testament. What similarities do you find between Aslan's covenant with certain animals in Narnia and God's covenanting with ancient Israel (Noah in Genesis 9; Abraham in Genesis 12; Moses in Exodus 19; and David in 2 Samuel 7)? What differences can you find? How does all of this compare with God's covenant in Christ with us (Heb 8–9)?

3   Lewis paints a vivid depiction of the power of temptation in the story of Digory and the forbidden fruit. While the offer of eternal life and the power to rule as king are of little temptation to him (though, presumably, they would have been quite tempting to others), the opportunity to heal his mother was a very real temptation. Does Aslan's response to Digory when asked about the promise of the forbidden fruit surprise you? Why or why not? What does Aslan's explanation reveal about our understanding of temptation and the false promises that sin makes?

THE LION, THE WITCH AND THE WARDROBE

SYNOPSIS & CHARACTERS

Perhaps the most well-known book of Lewis's Narnia series, *The Lion, the Witch and the Wardrobe* tells the story of the four Pevensie children, Peter, Susan, Edmund, and Lucy, who are sent to the country home of an old professor (Professor Kirke) during the World War II bombings of London. Once there, the children entertain themselves with games around the home. It is during a game of hide-and-seek that Lucy, the youngest, hides in a wardrobe, and stepping through several fur coats, finds herself in the snowy world of Narnia.

In Narnia, Lucy meets a faun by the name of Mr. Tumnus, who explains that the White Witch has cast a spell over the entire country of Narnia, leaving it "always winter but never Christmas." Leading the young Lucy to his home to warm up, he later reveals to Lucy that he was actually convinced by the White Witch to capture Lucy, but, after meeting her, he explains that he cannot go through with it (much to Lucy's relief).

Traveling back through the wardrobe, Lucy finds her siblings and explains all that she has experienced in Narnia—even though, curiously, it seems that no time has passed since she left. Edmund also travels to Narnia, and he finds himself face-to-face with the White Witch, who tempts Edmund with enchanted Turkish delight, and persuades him to return to Narnia with his siblings in exchange for the promise of being made a prince.

When the four Pevensie children enter Narnia together, they meet Mr. and Mrs. Beaver, two speaking animals who tell the girls and boys of Aslan the lion. Aslan is the true "king of the Wood," the children are told, even though the White Witch has reigned over the perpetual-winter land of Narnia for the past century. More importantly, the Pevensie children are told that Aslan is "on the move," and that he is preparing an uprising to overthrow the White Witch.

Edmund soon sneaks off to catch up with the White Witch and receive his reward, but her evil motives are unveiled, and he is captured. Peter, Susan, and Lucy join sides with the animals true to Aslan and battle the White Witch's forces. When Jadis the White Witch reveals that she has a claim to Edmund's life because his betrayal broke the command written on the Stone Table, Aslan offers his own life in exchange for Edmund's. While the White Witch had planned to take Edmund's life as a way to overturn ancient prophecies that foretold that two Sons of Adam and two Daughters of Eve would overthrow the White Witch, this is an offer she cannot refuse. Aslan is thus killed in Edmund's place, to the great celebration of the White Witch's evil forces.

However, that is far from the end of Aslan. Aslan returns from the grave, explains to the children that "Deeper Magic," of which the White Witch was unaware, brought about his resurrection. The four children are then made kings and queens of Narnia; many years later, they accidentally make their way through the first wood and, then, the wardrobe. As they stumble back into the professor's home, they realize that although years passed during their Narnia adventures, it was as if no time had passed at all in our world.

BIBLICAL THEMES

In *The Lion, the Witch and the Wardrobe*, readers are introduced to many characters and themes that lay the foundation for and reappear throughout the other Narnia stories. Many of these themes not only help readers better understand the rest of the Narnia books, but also illuminate aspects of the Christian story. The two themes we'll explore here are the mixed responses to the person of Jesus Christ, and the account and meaning of his crucifixion and resurrection.

ASLAN AS JESUS CHRIST IN NARNIA

When asked about how readers should understand the relationship between Aslan the lion in Narnia and Jesus Christ of Scripture, Lewis offered the following suggestion: "Let us suppose that there were a land like Narnia and that the Son of God, as He became a Man in our world, became a Lion there, and then imagine what would have happened" (Lewis's May 29, 1954, letter to a fifth-grade classroom). There is, then, not a one-to-one relationship between the Christ of Scripture and the lion of Narnia. And yet, it does appear that Lewis did his best to imagine what the same Word-become-flesh would be like if he were incarnate in Narnia. By reading Aslan in this way, what we find is not a temptation toward idolatry—as though we might worship Aslan—but, instead, an opportunity to see the Christ of Scripture through a new set of eyes.

MIXED RESPONSES

In what ways might our reading of Aslan in *The Lion, the Witch and the Wardrobe* give a fresh understanding of the person of Jesus? First, note that those in the story don't have a universal, uniform response to Aslan, but a mixed response. Even before they know much about who Aslan is, the four Pevensie children respond differently when they first hear of the lion. As Professor Ash notes, at the name "Aslan," Edmund experiences "mysterious horror"— most likely reflecting his impending betrayal—while Peter is filled with deep courage. Susan is delighted—as though she's just tasted something delicious or heard a beautiful tune. Lucy has the feeling of waking up on the first day of summer holiday. Elsewhere, this scene is echoed in *The Magician's Nephew*, where Uncle Andrew and Jadis respond to Aslan's voice with horror and the urge to flee while the cabby responds to the same voice by claiming that if he had only known that such a voice existed, he would have been a better man.

This mixed response to Aslan parallels the variety of responses we find to those in Scripture who encounter Jesus. For every one who responds with joy, one responds in anger. Upon meeting Jesus as a young boy in the Jerusalem temple, Simeon declares that he can now die in peace, having received the promise that he would see the Messiah before he died (Luke 2:22-35). Years later, when Jesus reads from the book of Isaiah in the Nazareth synagogue on the Sabbath and declares that the text had been fulfilled in their presence, those in the synagogue are furious (Luke 4:14-30). When Jesus feeds thousands with little more than a boy's lunch, the crowd want to make him king (John 6:1-15). When the same crowd finds Jesus the next day and he tells them that unless they feed on him they will have no life in them, all of those present turn and leave until there are no more than a dozen left (John 6:25-71). A woman with a shameful past is so overwhelmed upon seeing Jesus that she washes his feet with her tears (Luke 7:36-38). When Jesus claims that he and the Father "are one," the response is the kind of anger that boils over with a desire to take Jesus' life (John 10:27-36). Jesus enters Jerusalem riding on a donkey during the week of Passover, and he is greeted by crowds covering the path with palm branches and their cloaks, lifting up their voices in shouts of joy and praise (Matt 21:1-11; Mark 11:1-11; Luke 19:28-44; John 12:12-19). Others present urge Jesus to rebuke the crowds for their response—not thinking Jesus' entrance is worth such a reception—and they are told that if the people were not to receive him with praise, creation itself would (Luke 19:40). In the final moments of his earthly life, hanging on a cross between two crucified thieves, the scourged and crucified Jesus is ridiculed on one side and defended on the other (Luke 23:39-43).

Encountering Jesus has always produced very different responses among the people portrayed in Scripture as well as among people around the world today. The fear and anger—as well as the absolute joy and deep courage—prompted by the very name of Aslan are also very real responses to the name, teaching, legacy, and person of Christ.

In what is a hopeful note in *The Lion, the Witch and the Wardrobe*, someone's initial negative response to Aslan need not be their final response. As has been noted, while the other Pevensie children respond with courage and delight at the sound of Aslan's name, Edmund is filled with terror. By the end of the story, however, Aslan and Edmund have a private conversation that, we are told, Edmund "never forgot." From that point on, Edmund's heart was committed to Aslan. Edmund's redemption story invites us into a posture of hope for any whose hearts are now hard, cold, or even angry at the name of Jesus.

FROM DEATH TO LIFE

Another biblical theme illuminated by *The Lion, the Witch and the Wardrobe* is the account of Jesus' death and resurrection. This event, so central to the Christian tradition, is paralleled in the story of Aslan's murder at the hand of the White Witch.

It's a portrait of ultimate self-surrender: in Chapter 14 of *The Lion, the Witch and the Wardrobe*, Susan and Lucy find Aslan walking in the dead of night. The children notice Aslan does not seem like himself; the great lion appears lonely and sad, even in their company. When they reach the Stone Table, Aslan tells the children they must leave him; they go, but hide themselves behind a bush so that they can see what happens next. To their horror, Aslan is met by the White Witch and a horde of evil creatures. The White Witch orders the creatures to bind the lion and, though they are initially too afraid, Aslan's passive, apathetic posture leads the creatures to comply with her orders. The lion's beautiful mane is shaved; he is physically beaten; and he is mocked, all without any attempt to fight back. When Aslan is finally bound and laid on the Stone Table, the White Witch approaches with a stone knife, which she lifts high and thrusts into the lion's shaven fur.

With all hope of Aslan rescuing Narnia from the Witch seemingly lost, Susan and Lucy, crying, attend to Aslan's body. Indeed, overwrought with anguish, they can do no more than sit and mourn. But just then, they are shocked to hear a loud, cracking noise behind them. Turning to find the source, the two girls notice the giant Stone Table has been cracked from top to bottom, and they are stunned to find Aslan standing before them, returned from death to life. To show that he is neither a dream nor a ghost, the resurrected Aslan breathes his warm breath on Susan and Lucy. He goes on to explain the "Deeper Magic," which goes back to before the dawn of time and which promises that if a willing, innocent victim volunteers to die in place of a traitor, then death itself will work backward.

For those familiar with the account of Jesus' crucifixion and resurrection, this story from *The Lion, the Witch and the Wardrobe* seems all too familiar; the parallels are many and obvious. And yet, Lewis seems interested in far more than readers merely finding one-to-one parallels with the details of Jesus' passion. For those of us who have grown used to such a life-changing story after attending so many Easter services over the years, Lewis encourages us to feel the horror and beauty of this story anew. Can you sense the anguish Susan and Lucy must feel as they watch the horrific scene, wanting to cry out but feeling helpless? Does your heart sink with theirs when they weep over his dead body? And then, do you find your heart leaping at the sound of the resurrected Aslan's voice?

Does this telling of the "Deeper Magic" at work in Aslan's sacrificial death stir in you a deep sense of gratitude for Christ's own sacrifice for the world? Does the scene of the resurrected Aslan breathing the stone creatures to life fill you with joyful surprise and hope?

FOR REFLECTION

1   How should we think of the relationship between the Aslan of Narnia and the Jesus of Scripture? Was C. S. Lewis trying to say that Aslan is the Narnian equivalent to Jesus Christ? How might you explain this relationship to a Christian friend who has never read *The Lion, the Witch and the Wardrobe*? How might you explain this relationship to a non-Christian friend?

2   Aslan's voice creates different responses in different people. Why might this be? What, exactly, is the cause of the different response to the same figure? How have you seen this to be true of different people's responses to Jesus in your life?

3 How does the account of Aslan's death and resurrection in *The Lion, the Witch and the Wardrobe* lead you to think differently about Jesus' death and resurrection? Were you to use this story from *The Lion, the Witch and the Wardrobe* in a Holy Week devotion, what would you encourage readers to focus their attention on? What character would you linger on? Even now, which emotion illustrated in this scene do you most resonate with?

THE LAST BATTLE

SYNOPSIS & CHARACTERS

We now turn to the final book in this video: the last story in the Narnia series, and what Professor Ash refers to as his favorite among all the Narnia chronicles. Published in 1956, *The Last Battle* tells the story of the end of Narnia and the entrance into the true Narnia.

The book begins hundreds of years after the last Aslan sighting. Taking advantage of those waiting for Aslan's return, an ape by the name of Shift dresses up a donkey named Puzzle in a lion's skin and fools others into thinking that Aslan has returned. While the animals gather around a stable to witness the false Aslan, a foreign enemy, Calormen, takes the opportunity to invade Narnia. Soon after, the Narnian king is captured, and he cries out to the children of earth for help. In response, Eustace Scrubb (from *The Voyage of the Dawn Treader* and *The Silver Chair*) and Jill Pole (from *The Silver Chair*) arrive in Narnia to help fight against the Calormenes on behalf of Narnia.

When they free Puzzle and unveil that he is not actually Aslan, the children realize that the stable where Puzzle was led out each night is now being presided over by Tash, the evil deity of the Calormenes. As a result, the stable becomes very dangerous—those who go in are eaten. Shift the ape, after becoming a mouthpiece for the Calormenes, decides to enter the stable to see Tash and is devoured.

A battle between Narnia's forces and the Calormenes ensues around the stable, with each side trying to force the other into the stable. When the Narnians enter, they are surprised to find the true Aslan there. Rather than dark, it is now light—and far bigger than they could have imagined from the outside. Aslan commands Tash to depart, and soon those who remain are joined by the seven kings and queens of Narnia: Peter, Edmund, Lucy, Digory, Polly, Eustace, and Jill. The one missing queen is Susan, who, the reader is told, is "no longer a friend of Narnia."

At this point, Aslan stands at the door of the stable, and everyone present passes either into darkness or into glorious splendor. Those who pass into the dark are never seen again. Those who pass into the light, on the other hand, enter the true, heavenly Narnia, of which the old Narnia was only ever a shadow. Everything that they had experienced in Narnia was merely preparation, or an introduction, to what they are now beginning to experience as they move "further up and further in."

BIBLICAL THEMES

The Last Battle includes a number of biblical themes worth exploring; these center mostly on the doctrine of eschatology, or last things. We will focus on two: the final judgment, and salvation for those outside of Christianity.

Final Judgment: Susan's Conspicuous Absence

In one of the most powerful parallels between the biblical texts and the Narnia series, we find Aslan standing in the seat of judgment at the end of *The Last Battle*—a scene worth exploring in greater depth. One of the most startling aspects of this scene is Susan Pevensie's absence. For many readers, young and old, Susan's absence—and Aslan's explanation—not only hurts, but leaves much to be desired. I once met a woman who, decades after growing up on the Narnia series, was still holding a grudge against C. S. Lewis for this literary decision!

But the emotions around Susan's fate involve much more than just a literary decision. Susan's absence suggests that she is missing out on the glory of Narnia that the others are entering into—and as a result of her enjoyment of nylons, lipstick, and party invitations over Narnia, no less! Many readers have wondered how Lewis could condemn Susan to hell for enjoying the kind of things most girls of her age would enjoy.

In response to such a critical view of Susan's fate, C. S. Lewis consoled one young reader in a 1957 letter: "The books don't tell us what happened to Susan. She is left alive in this world at the end, having by then turned into a rather silly, conceited young woman. But there's plenty of time for her to mend and perhaps she will get to Aslan's country in the end ... in her own way." While many who read *The Last Battle* see Susan's absence as a sour ending to the beloved Narnia chronicles, Lewis in this letter appears to suggest that this need not reflect her final state. So what, then, is Lewis saying through Susan's absence?

Contrary to those who suggest that Lewis was a curmudgeonly old man who shuns the simple pleasures of many well-meaning young women, Lewis seems interested specifically in the temptation to put earthly desires before the concerns of God's kingdom. Far from putting the blame on young women or even feminine pleasures in general, this is a warning for all of us: no one is beyond the temptation to get so caught up in our earthly activities that we lose sight of our true home and that which promises to satisfy truly. Such a temptation, rather than any specifically feminine critique, is what Lewis is here warning against at the end of the Narnia series.

This is a warning that Jesus himself makes in the parable of the sower (Mark 4:1–20; Matthew 13:1–23; Luke 8:1–15). In this parable, Jesus tells of seed that falls on good soil, but when it begins to grow, thorns choke it, and as a result, it does not bear fruit. According to Jesus' explanation of the parable, this seed represents those who hear the word of God but who are soon led away by the cares of this world. Such would-be believers are no longer fruit-bearing representatives of God's kingdom; they are choked out of the good, life-giving word God entrusted to them as his representatives. This, it would seem, is what Lewis describes through Susan's character at the end of *The Last Battle*.

And yet, it is worth pointing out that Lewis in no way condemns Susan. At the end of the book, Susan remains alive on earth (unlike the other Pevensie children, who were killed in a tragic British Railway accident), and so she has every opportunity to return to the way of life and the signs she experienced in Narnia, to trust them as the true reality and not the "childish fantasy" she now deems them. Susan's fate is not sealed; nor is her fate known to us, but to God alone. There is still time, Lewis emphasizes for Susan as much as for all of us, to live into the reality of God's kingdom.

SALVATION FOR NON-CHRISTIANS

Another common question readers ask at the conclusion of the Narnia series: What about those who aren't Aslan's followers? Might some of them, too, enter through the stable door into the glory of true Narnia? Lewis answers with a resounding "Yes!"

In a surprising turn for Emeth (a Calormene who has followed the foreign god Tash all of his life), in Chapter 15 Aslan welcomes the Calormene into his blessed glory after Tash's defeat. Like Emeth at the end of *The Last Battle*, many readers are surprised to find that the good news of Aslan's triumphant return and ultimate reign extends to those we would not think of as Aslan's followers. While we have already said that we ought not read a direct, one-to-one application of Aslan's works in Narnia to Christ's works in ours, this scene does leave readers wondering what this might mean for what Lewis believed about the salvation of those outside of Christianity.

People's views on the relationship between salvation, Christianity, and world religions tend to fall into three general categories: pluralism, which suggests that all religious traditions ultimately provide equally valid means to God and his salvation; inclusivism, which claims that although the Christ event is the unique site of God's salvation, salvation is still possible for non-Christians;

and exclusivism, which states that only those who hear and respond to the "good news" of the Christian message will receive God's salvation.

With these categories in mind, we might ask how best to understand Lewis's view of salvation for those outside of the Christian tradition. Can we read Lewis as a pluralist, suggesting that all religions ultimately say the same thing and that all roads lead to the same place? This is the question Emeth poses to Aslan: "Lord, is it then true, as the Ape said, that thou and Tash are One? The Lion growled so that the earth shook ... and said, It is false" (Chapter 15). Aslan's earth-shaking response makes clear that Aslan and Tash are not equally valid ways into the true Narnia. As Aslan explains to Emeth, Tash and Aslan could not be further from each other— they are opposites. Nor are Christ and the gods of other religions equally valid ways to the same heavenly reality.

Lewis's views on the centrality of the Christ event, here in Narnia as well as in other writings, prevent us from identifying his views with pluralism, which leaves us with either inclusivism or exclusivism. Reflecting on this question, Lewis scholar Dr. Jerry Root notes, "Unlike his mentor George MacDonald, [Lewis] did not believe that all will be saved, but he did speculate that the door to heaven may be opened for some who follow other religions."[2] As Dr. Root notes, it seems Lewis could fit well in the inclusivism category: perhaps Christ's salvific work is so great and so broad that it reaches even those outside of the Christian faith.

Such an interpretation of the relationship between Jesus, salvation, and those outside of Christianity finds support in Jesus' own words when he tells his disciples: "And I have other sheep that are not of this fold. I must bring them also, and they will listen to my voice. So there will be one flock, one shepherd" (John 10:16). According to this view, Jesus remains the only way to salvation (John 14:6), but his call may very well reach beyond those whom we would typically recognize as his own.

FOR REFLECTION

1 In *The Last Battle*, the wicked ape Shift dresses up the donkey named Puzzle in an animal skin and leads others to believe that Puzzle is the royal lion Aslan, returned to Narnia. Apparently he even deceives some, who come out and begin to honor the false Aslan as they might Aslan himself. How might this scene help us better understand the character of the antichrist in Scripture? For reflection, you might refer to these biblical texts: Daniel 7:25; 2 Thessalonians 2:3-4; and 1 John 2:18.

2 Many Narnia readers who reach the end of the series are disturbed by Susan's absence from the children's entrance into true Narnia—particularly when Aslan explains why. How might you respond to such concerns? Does this mean she is condemned to hell? Why or why not?

3 Though he is a Calormene and is described as worshiping Tash all his life, Emeth is welcomed by Aslan into the glory of true Narnia. Does this suggest that all roads provide equally valid ways to the true Narnia? Does Aslan even matter? Further, what might this suggest about the salvation of those outside of Christianity?

NARNIA, PART II

THE HORSE AND HIS BOY

IN THE PREVIOUS EPISODE, PROFESSOR ASH INTRODUCED US TO "The Big Three" books in the Narnia Chronicles: *The Magician's Nephew*; *The Lion, the Witch and the Wardrobe*; and *The Last Battle*. In this video, we will be introduced to the four remaining books, beginning with *The Horse and His Boy*.

SYNOPSIS & CHARACTERS

Published in 1954 as the fifth book in the Narnia series, *The Horse and His Boy* begins with the Pevensie children not in our world, but already in Narnia. Set after their coronation in *The Lion, the Witch and the Wardrobe* but prior to their return to England at the book's conclusion, *The Horse and His Boy* takes place during the time of the four Pevensie children's reign in Narnia. However, they are not the story's main characters. That role is reserved for four new characters: a young boy named Shasta and a talking horse, Bree, who meet a young woman named Aravis and her horse, Hwin. These characters are united in their attempt to flee Calormen— a hot, massive country to the south of Narnia with a great army.

Shasta escapes to avoid a life of slavery, while Aravis is avoiding a forced marriage.

On their journey north to Narnia in pursuit of freedom, however, they encounter trouble. In Tashbaan, Calormen's high-walled capital, the main characters meet two Narnian rulers, King Edmund and Queen Susan. There, too, Shasta is mistaken for royalty—he bears an uncanny resemblance to Corin, a prince of Archenland, the country bordering both Calormen and Narnia. Like Aravis, Queen Susan herself is fleeing a marriage proposal, this one from Prince Rabadash of Calormen.

When Aravis learns of Prince Rabadash's plans to invade Archenland and Narnia to the north—in hopes of making Susan his queen—she and Aravis set off on their horses to warn those in Archenland of the pending trouble. En route, the four characters encounter a lion (who they later realize is Aslan), who motivates them to speed up their travels. When they reach Archenland, Prince Rabadash and his forces are not far behind. A battle soon ensues, and it is unclear who will prove victorious until the Narnian forces from the north arrive and help Archenland defeat the Calormenes. As it turns out, Shasta is actually the elder twin of Prince Corin of Archenland; taking his original name, Cor, he succeeds his father to the throne of Archenland and fulfills the prophecy that he would save Archenland from defeat. Aravis and Cor marry at the book's conclusion (so as to quarrel and make up more conveniently, we're told), as do the talking horses Bree and Hwin (though not each other).

BIBLICAL THEMES

While explicit parallels between the story of The Horse and His Boy and the Bible are not as apparent as in the other Narnia stories we've discussed, this book—like the others—contains important biblical themes worth exploring, particularly as they relate to our spiritual growth. Both of the themes we'll consider involve the issue of pride, though they concern pride in different forms.

PRIDE AS SELF-IMPORTANCE

The first theme we'll explore is pride as a form of overinflated self-importance, illustrated by Prince Rabadash's response to his capture by Archenland's ruler, King Lune. Though Rabadash is offered a conditional release, he refuses, driven by his own arrogance. Even while he remains captive, Rabadash continues to heckle and taunt not only his captors but Aslan, as well. When he refuses to heed Aslan's warning to hold his tongue, Rabadash is turned into a donkey, causing all those present to erupt into laughter. Aslan informs Rabadash that he need not remain a donkey forever, however. As Rabadash appealed to his foreign god Tash, Aslan commands Rabadash to return to Calormen and the temple of Tash in order to be healed. However, if he ventures more than ten miles from the temple, he will return to donkey form, never again to be healed.

As Professor Ash notes, Rabadash's error is his arrogance. Even when it is clear that he is powerless and must admit the power of his captors, Rabadash holds onto his own self-perceived importance and power. By refusing to acknowledge his own helplessness, Rabadash makes an ass of himself quite literally.

The twin themes of humility and pride are not of minor importance to Lewis. We already noted in our study of *Mere Christianity* that, for Lewis, pride is the chief of all sins; it makes it impossible to see God (see Chapter 8, Book 3, *Mere Christianity*). What is

needed for humans in relation to God, Lewis repeatedly emphasizes, is to realize our total inadequacy and utter dependence on
God. However, such a posture is impossible so long as we operate
from a position of self-assumed importance or arrogance. This
quite clearly is Rabadash's sin. But humility is not an optional
virtue for Christians. It is absolutely essential to the Christian life.

Eventually, Prince Rabadash is freed from his donkey form,
as he remains in Calormen's capital, which results not only in his
own freedom from pride but also in peace with the surround-
ing countries.

Pride as Intellectual Arrogance

Like Rabadash, the speaking horse Bree wrestles with pride—
though in a different form. As a prized Calormene steed, Bree
apparently developed a high view of himself. He prides himself
in his knowledge, going even so far as to discount the reality of a
literal Aslan. At one point, Bree explains that when Narnians speak
of Aslan, they are not speaking of a *real* lion, but only an analogy that is meant to emphasize the traits of a lion, such as great
strength. Bree laughs off any claims of a literal Aslan as befitting
a child's imagination.

At just that moment, Bree, Hwin, and Aravis bump into Aslan
himself. After a brief pause, Hwin steps toward Aslan, fearing
that she may be eaten but saying that even if she were to be eaten
by Aslan, it would be better than to remain apart from him. Aslan
praises her for this response of faith.

Bree, by contrast, is rebuked for standing off and refusing
to come to Aslan. Whereas Rabadash's pride stemmed from an
overinflated sense of self-importance, Bree's pride is a form of

intellectual arrogance. Blinded by his own pride, Bree had been unable to accept that Aslan could be a true, literal king. However, when brought face-to-face with Aslan, in a scene reminiscent of Thomas's encounter with the resurrected Jesus (John 20:20–29), Bree does eventually step forward and experience the literal Aslan for himself. The great lion's true identity is now made apparent, and Bree is freed from the grip of his intellectual pride. He now knows that Aslan is no mere myth or analogy, but true flesh and blood—and more.

Similarly, John's Gospel notes that after Thomas sees the crucified, resurrected Jesus for himself and is invited to put his finger in Jesus' side, Thomas speaks a confident word of faith: "My Lord and my God!" (John 20:28). Thomas's doubts concerning Jesus' literal resurrection fall away in response to seeing and touching the Lord for himself.

Of course, not all of us are so fortunate as to be able to experience the resurrected Jesus in the flesh and blood. Knowing this, Jesus spoke an assuring word: "Have you believed because you have seen me? Blessed are those who have not seen and yet have believed" (John 20:29). Even though those of us living in the time between Jesus' ascension and return are unable to see and touch the resurrected Son of God for ourselves just yet, we, too, are called to place our faith and hope in the literal person of Jesus Christ as Messiah and Son of God. Jesus describes the lives of those who do as blessed.

FOR REFLECTION

1 When given the opportunity to admit defeat and agree to his own conditional release, Rabadash continues to heckle his

captors and refuse to acknowledge his own need for help—even when Aslan promises that trouble will come his way if he doesn't relent. In this scene, Lewis not only illustrates the very practical captivity we all face when it comes to our own overinflated sense of self-importance, but also the way in which pride's grip removes us from living Christ's commands. Give an example of either the practical constraints pride has placed on your life, or how pride has kept you back from heeding Christ's call on your life.

2 In the scene of Bree laughing off the idea of a literal Aslan, C. S. Lewis illustrates the dangers of intellectual arrogance, which can blind us to experiencing the reality of Christ as the literal, resurrected Messiah and Son of God. Lewis himself lived and worked in a setting recognized as one of the great intellectual epicenters of the world; he would have encountered people who shunned belief in a literal Jesus Christ as childish. Describe a time when intellectual arrogance prevented you or someone you know from accepting a traditional, orthodox understanding of Jesus's life, death, and resurrection. How did you respond? What might be helpful in such a situation?

3   After Thomas acknowledges Jesus as "my Lord and my God," what sort of blessing do you think Jesus meant when he said, "Blessed are those who have not seen and yet have believed" (John 20:28–29)?

SECTION TWO

PRINCE CASPIAN

A s Professor Ash notes, C. S. Lewis once described the story of *Prince Caspian* as the "restoration of true religion after corruption" (March 5, 1961, letter to Anne Jenkins). The corruption of true religion is illustrated by the fall of Narnia, introduced at the outset of this book. *Prince Caspian* begins with the four Pevensie children at a train platform in England one year after their first adventures in Narnia, which amounts to more than 1,000 years in Narnia time. During this time, Narnia has fallen to ruins, and the children are called back to rescue it.

Upon arriving in Narnia once again and seeing Cair Paravel in ruins, Trumpkin the dwarf informs the Pevensie children that the Telmarines now rule over Narnia. It soon becomes clear that Prince Caspian was the one who used Susan's magical horn to call the Pevensies back to Narnia in hopes that they might help rescue the land from Miraz, Caspian's uncle and current king of Narnia. Under the Telmarines' reign, the old creatures of Narnia retreated to the woods, awaiting Aslan's return. Caspian's teacher, Dr. Cornelius, revealed to Caspian that Miraz tried to cover up

all of the old ways of Narnia in hopes that they would be forgotten. Further, he also concealed Caspian's rightful role as Narnia's
king. When Miraz's wife, Queen Prunaprismia, gave birth to a
son, Caspian learned of Miraz's plan to kill Caspian to ensure his
own son's reign. Caspian fled to the woods; there, he met the creatures of old Narnia in hiding and called on the Pevensie children
by way of a magical horn in order to help stage a coup and return
Narnia to its old ways.

Once joined with the Pevensies, Caspian leads the old Narnians
to Aslan's How, the site of the ancient Stone Table from *The Lion,
the Witch and the Wardrobe*, where the rebel forces are being gath-
ered. The Telmarines, however, are not the only forces they must
face; a dwarf named Nikabrik had begun to tell others that Aslan
no longer existed and, even worse, attempts to call the White
Witch back to life.

Eventually, those who are true to old Narnia, aided by the
Pevensie children and Aslan himself, overpower not only Nikabrik's
evil plot but Miraz as well. When Peter Pevensie challenges Miraz
to a duel, Miraz is defeated not by Peter's swift shot but by two of
his own soldiers. With Miraz's defeat, Aslan appoints Caspian true
king of Narnia, and the Pevensie children are returned to the train
platform from which they had previously been beckoned by the
magical horn's blow, as if they had never left.

BIBLICAL THEMES

Prince Caspian includes a number of scenes that poignantly display many important themes for those hoping to grow in their
Christian life. We will explore two here: what it looks like to possess bold faith in the midst of great challenges, and the Christian
response to God's seemingly delayed return.

BOLD FAITH

As Professor Ash notes in this video, even though she is the youngest of the Pevensie children, Lucy displays great faith throughout the Narnia series. That is especially true in this story of *Prince Caspian*. After being called back into Narnia, the children are joined by Trumpkin the dwarf, and they are soon on their way to join forces with Caspian and the old Narnians. Finding their allies, however, is no easy task. At one point in their journey, the four Pevensie children and Trumpkin come to a great gorge and are unsure which way to pass in order to journey forward—should they go up, choosing the more difficult path, or should they journey down? It is at this fork in the road that Lucy—and only Lucy—spots Aslan calling her to travel up, not down, as the others had been suggesting they go. But since Lucy is the only one who sees Aslan, the others take a vote and decide to take the easier route. Following the other children and Trumpkin, Lucy weeps bitterly.

Later in the journey Lucy once again encounters Aslan, this time in a quiet, moonlit wood, while the other children are fast asleep. After a joyful reunion, Aslan silently scolds Lucy for not listening to him when he had so clearly revealed the direction they were to travel. Eventually, Lucy is emboldened by Aslan to return to the children and once again encourage them to go forward, in faith, on the path Aslan revealed. Lucy's conversation with Aslan paints a powerful portrait of bold, courageous obedience for Christians everywhere, of all ages.

Contrary to some contemporary distortions of the Christian life as an always-enjoyable, easy journey with great material blessing, following Christ is a costly path that he leads us on. Jesus himself encourages his would-be followers to count the cost before coming after him (Luke 14:25–35). Similar to Lucy's own experience in *Prince Caspian*, anyone who names Jesus as Lord will inevitably come to a fork in the road and have to choose between staying true to the path they know Christ to be leading them on—even if it comes at a great cost—or succumb to the pressures that abound to take another, easier path.

Lucy's encounter with Aslan serves as a helpful model of one who experiences Christ's leading and is tasked with leading others down a revealed path—even if it comes at great cost. In the face of such a frightening call, Lucy has several concerns, which she raises to Aslan (Chapter 10). First, what if she goes to the other children to share this word of his leading, and they don't believe her? Aslan replies that the most important thing is that Lucy is true to Aslan's leading, regardless of others' response. She must not be persuaded against what she knows to be true simply because others do not believe her. Further, she must not waste time wondering how things would have turned out had she followed Aslan's leading in the past. The important thing, Aslan encourages her, is that she listen *now*, rather than wondering what would have been.

But Lucy's fears do not end there. Lucy asks if Aslan would have liked her to follow him even if it meant her, and her alone, taking that route. What if others not only do not believe her—what if they refuse to follow? Aslan's response is unflinching: "If they will not, then you at least must follow me alone." The difficult lesson in this story is that faithful pursuit of Christ can be a lonely pursuit. As German pastor-theologian Dietrich Bonhoeffer noted in the opening chapter of his classic work *Life Together*, Christian community is a privilege and a gift of God that not every Christian will

experience in this life. At many points along the Christian journey, the path will be deeply lonely. Others will not always join us
in pursuing Christ where his voice leads. And yet, the important
thing, as noted in this story, is that we continue to follow where he
leads, even if it means traveling alone. As we continue to pursue
Christ, we will find ourselves growing in him. Even when the road
grows long and hard, our perspective will be such that he will
seem bigger and fuller than we previously knew him to be—just
as Aslan seemed to grow larger to Lucy, though, really, it was she
who was growing.

Doubting Aslan's Return

Another scene in *Prince Caspian* that reveals a deeply important
biblical theme for Christian growth is the scene where Caspian
and the old Narnians must wait in the faith that the four Pevensie
children and Aslan will come to their rescue. After blowing Susan's
magical horn and still not seeing any sight of the children or Aslan,
however, they begin to lose faith. It is at this point that the dwarf
Nikabrik voices great doubt in Aslan: "Either Aslan is dead, or
he is not on our side. Or else something stronger than himself
keeps him back. And if he did come—how do we know he'd be our
friend?" (Chapter 12).

   With no sign of the Pevensies or Aslan in sight, Nikabrik dis-
credits faith in Aslan. Perhaps none of the stories were more than
mere myth. Referring to the stories of Aslan returning to life again
after being slain by the White Witch, Nikabrik casts doubt on these
tales: "We hear precious little about anything he did afterwards. ...
How do you explain that, if he really came to life?" Nikabrik goes
on to suggest that they ought to take matters into their own hands,

even if it means calling on the White Witch and her evil powers for their own help.

This story is a poignant reflection of our own contemporary temptation to begin to lose hope in the stories of Christ's life, death, and resurrection, and his eventual return. When the painful, harsh reality of daily news paints a seemingly worsening picture of our world—plagued as it is by disease, poverty, and sociopolitical oppression—we can be tempted to lose hope in the renewal of all things in Christ's return. This is precisely the issue for Nikabrik, who concluded that Aslan did not actually exist or, if he did, he either did not care or was simply powerless to help. As Caspian explains, Nikabrik's disillusionment was understood only in response to so much darkness: "He had gone sour inside from long suffering and hating." In light of so much suffering, it can be tempting to begin to think that any true change must come not from Christ's work, but from our own. Such was Nikabrik's pragmatic response to Aslan's absence: he was willing to turn even to evil as a last resort.

This story has two important lessons for Christians. First, our response to a suffering world must maintain a full, committed confidence in Christ's past work and future in-breaking kingdom. Even when others begin to doubt the stories of Jesus' life, death, and resurrection, Christians must not. As was the case when so many others began to lose hope in Jesus, so, too, must we respond like Peter: "Lord, to whom shall we go? You have the words of eternal life" (John 6:68). Second, in addition to holding fast to our confidence in Christ in the midst of so much darkness, Christians are also called to embody the kind of life native to God's kingdom in our own present day. Christian hope is never passive, but always active. Even though God's kingdom will only ever be instantiated by God and not our own efforts, Christians are called to live into the reality of that new way of life now.

The lesson from this story of Nikabrik in *Prince Caspian* is that even when all appearances might suggest an otherwise absent or aloof God, Christians are called not to naïve hope, but to confident trust in the life, death, and resurrection of our Lord Jesus Christ and to proactive embodiment of the kind of faithful life witnessed in Christ (Matthew 5–7), which will be brought to full fruition upon his return.

FOR REFLECTION

1   Lucy's encounter with Aslan in *Prince Caspian*, as we have discussed, is a helpful model for what it looks like to follow Christ with bold faith. But embodying such faith is no easy task, particularly when others challenge, laugh at, or ignore Jesus' leading. How might we explain to others, who perhaps have not experienced Jesus' leading in their own life, why we would follow the more difficult path when it goes against good reason? Further, how might we be encouraged to continue on the path we know Christ to be calling us on, even if it means venturing on alone?

2   In the face of great pain and suffering in our world, Christians can be tempted to respond in one of two ways: to believe that any efforts to respond to the world's injustices would be futile since God will ultimately restore and reconcile creation in Jesus' final return, or to believe that we must take matters into our own hands. Why are both of these responses misguided? How does Nikabrik's response to Aslan's delay help us understand what faithfulness to Christ looks like in the already-not-yet period between Christ's ascension and final return?

THE VOYAGE OF THE DAWN TREADER

THE STORY OF *THE VOYAGE OF THE DAWN TREADER*, WHICH C. S. Lewis once described as the journey of the spiritual life, begins with two of the Pevensie children, Edmund and Lucy, and their cousin—a spoiled, bully of a boy named Eustace Scrubb. Lucy and Edmund are visiting Eustace when they are sucked into Narnia through a picture of a ship hanging on the wall of Eustace's parents' home. They are taken to Caspian's ship, the *Dawn Treader*, which is bound for the East, where Caspian hopes to find seven lost Narnian lords who had been sent off by Miraz (in *Prince Caspian*). They are joined by a chivalrous mouse named Reepicheep who hopes to find Aslan's country. One distinguishing mark of *The Voyage of the Dawn Treader* in the Narnia series is that it lacks a central antagonist. Instead, the central characters face a series of challenges on their journey, many of which test their own unique character flaws. On their voyage to find the seven lords, they encounter a number of exciting adventures and challenges, including Eustace finding a hoard of treasure and becoming a dragon; a magic pool that turns everything to gold and tempts

Caspian; the curious Dufflepud creatures and their wizard ruler, Coriakin; an island where dreams come to life; and three Narnian lords who are caught in an enchanted sleep, and who are guarded by Ramandu, a resting star.

At the end of their journey to the East, the ship can sail no further, so Lucy, Edmund, Eustace, and Reepicheep continue on in a small boat to the End of the World. Reepicheep eventually travels on his own to Aslan's country, "quivering with happiness," whereas the three children unknowingly meet Aslan in the form of a lamb that invites them to join it for breakfast on the shore. The lamb is soon revealed to be Aslan, who tells the children that they have been brought here so that they might learn to enter Aslan's country from their own world, before returning to Eustace's parents' home in England.

BIBLICAL THEMES

While there are a variety of biblical themes worth exploring in the story of *The Voyage of the Dawn Treader*, we will focus on just two: Eustace's conversion and Reepicheep's relentless pursuit of Aslan's country.

EUSTACE'S CONVERSION

In one of the most vivid scenes of the entire Narnia series, young Eustace Scrubb is brought face-to-face with his greed in a powerful way on the second island they visit. Wandering off from the rest of the bunch, Eustace stumbles upon a dragon's lair overflowing with treasure. Filling his pockets and dressing in as much treasure as he can manage, Eustace eventually falls asleep on a pile of coins. When he awakes to a pain in his arm, Eustace is horrified to find that he has transformed into a dragon!

When he manages to find the rest of the group, Eustace the dragon is overwhelmed to the point of tears and eventually persuades them not to attack him. Eustace begins to lose hope that he will ever be transformed back into a boy until, one evening, he meets a lion surrounded by a great light. The lion leads dragon-Eustace toward a pool where he is to bathe—but Eustace must first disrobe himself from his dragon skin. Using one of his own claws, Eustace tears his dragon skin away and attempts to enter the pool, only to realize another layer of dragon skin remains. This process repeats itself several times before it becomes clear that Eustace will need the lion's help. Lying flat on his back, Eustace is overwhelmed by a sharper pain than he has ever experienced when the lion's claw pierces his skin, but soon he is freed from thick, dark, knobby dragon form and is able to enter the waters to bathe. When he exits the bath, Eustace the boy is dressed in new clothes by the lion. It is only in recounting this story to Edmund that Eustace realizes his transformation is thanks to Aslan. Not only is his outward appearance transformed, but Eustace finds himself apologizing for treating others so "beastly."

There are several important points to draw out of this imaginative story, particularly as it relates to Christian conversion. The first is that true conversion is not ultimately achieved by our own efforts, but by Christ's work in our life. Just as Eustace's efforts to free himself from his beastly form proved futile—even when he was sure it had worked "this time"—so, too, are we unable to free ourselves from our own sinful ways. Eustace must first recognize his own inability to save himself before he finally ceases his own efforts and allows Aslan to do the most difficult work on his behalf. Though he cannot achieve this transformation on his own, it is his choice to allow the lion to work on his behalf, for his own good. So, too, for us: we can either choose to accept Christ's saving work in our life or hold him at arm's length. The hardest bit—our transformation—is Christ's work, but we must move toward him to receive it.

Another point worth noting in this story is the pain Eustace first feels when Aslan begins the work of his transformation. Unlike his own attempts to free himself from his dragon form, Aslan's work in his life comes with great pain. As Aslan's claw pierces his knobby dragon skin, Eustace says the pain is "worse than anything I've ever felt." The only thing that allows him to bear it is the freedom he feels. Much like the tearing of his dragon skin, Eustace's entrance into the bathing waters also bring a great pain, but they last for only a moment. Soon, he is swimming and splashing, freed not only from his dragon form, but also from the pain in his arm—from a gold band that had grown tight in his dragon transformation—that had first awoken him. For those who come to Christ, the transformation can also be painful at first, be it in terms of harmful practices or even relationships that must be given up. Similar to Eustace's experience of Aslan's penetrating claws, the author of Hebrews describes the encounter with God's word as piercing: "For the word of God is living and active, sharper than any two-edged sword, piercing to the division of soul and of spirit, of joints and of marrow, and discerning the thoughts and intentions of the heart" (Hebrews 4:12). However, what at first seems only painful soon brings great relief. I was recently speaking with a young man who confessed to me his five-year struggle with a pornography addiction. Even as he confessed the stranglehold it had had on his life for so long—which he enjoyed as much as he resented—his eyes grew wide with delight in confessing to me the freedom and joy he now found in no longer living in this former way of life. Such is the freedom those in Christ find, though it can be difficult and even painful at first.

Another detail in this story is the presence of water. The painful removal of Eustace's former way of life, pictured in his dragon form, is not enough, it seems. Before Aslan can dress him in new clothes, Eustace must enter the crystal-clear bathing waters. While views of the role of baptism in the Christian life differ across denominations, what they all uphold is that this practice is an identifying mark of Christians. Just as it was for the early Christians, baptism marks us as those who have been called into new life by Christ.

Lastly, this story notes that when Eustace is first freed from his dragon form, he is very tender underneath. And later, after he has come up out of the bathing waters, he needs to be dressed in new clothes by Aslan. As was the case with Eustace, there is a period in the life of new Christians where they are very tender, indeed. Though they have been welcomed into the new life that Christ offers, their former ways of life can still be tempting. Such new converts must be surrounded, supported, and encouraged by the loving community of the church, particularly as they are confronted with temptations to return to their former desires.

Again, similar to Eustace's experience in being clothed by Aslan, the apostle Paul described the practice of baptism as putting on Christ as one would put on a new set of clothes: "For all of you who were baptized into Christ have clothed yourselves with Christ" (Galatians 3:27 NIV). Those who are in Christ will look different—not merely by their own efforts, but by way of Christ's work in their life. For Eustace, his transformation was visibly noticeable not only in terms of his outward appearance but also in terms of his attitude. Indeed, at the conclusion of the book, we read that everyone back home notices Eustace's transformation. The takeaway? Those who have been baptized in Christ ought to look, sound, and act different. One indicator of Christ's life-changing transformation is the presence of the "fruit of the Spirit": "love, joy, peace, patience, kindness, goodness, faithfulness, gentleness, self-control" (Gal 5:22–23). While some of these traits are found even in those who are not following Christ, their consistent appearance in the life of a disciple is a reminder that change takes place when one comes to know Jesus as Lord. And the transformation will often be both dramatic and welcome.

REEPICHEEP'S RELENTLESS PURSUIT OF ASLAN'S COUNTRY

Arguably one of the most popular characters in the entire Narnia series, the chivalrous mouse Reepicheep stands out as a representation of a committed life of faith in *The Voyage of the Dawn Treader*. Reepicheep first appears in *Prince Caspian*, but the "chivalrous mice" created by the young C. S. Lewis in his fictional stories of Animal Land undoubtedly foreshadowed the Narnian mouse (see *Surprised by Joy*).

Standing on his hind legs, wearing a gold ring and a long crimson feather in his ear, speaking with great honor and chivalrous tones, a sword ready at his side, Reepicheep is a veritable portrait of medieval heroism in mouse form. Introduced early in *The Voyage of the Dawn Treader*, Reepicheep declares his intentions to sail on to Aslan's country in the far East. Reepicheep goes on to tell the others of how a verse was spoken over his life when he was a child;

in it, he was told that "to find all you seek, / There is the utter East." He confesses that although he isn't sure what its significance is, it has proved a guiding force in his life (Chapter 2). This prophetic word spoken over Reepicheep would prove true, but Reepicheep seems motivated by more than just a drive to fulfill the prophecy. As Professor Ash notes, it is his love for and commitment to Aslan that drives Reepicheep eastward. Where does this committed love for Aslan come from? When Reepicheep loses his tail in battle at the end of *Prince Caspian*, and when his fellow mice stand at the ready to cut off their own tails so that he wouldn't have to bear such shame alone, Aslan restored Reepicheep's tail. It was also Aslan who reminded Reepicheep that his dignity and honor are far too great to be placed in his tail (or outward appearances, for that matter). Reepicheep cannot forget Aslan's redemptive work in his life—and nothing, it seems, will stand in Reepicheep's way of reaching Aslan's country (Chapter 14).

Reepicheep's unwavering commitment to reaching Aslan and Aslan's country, no matter the perils on his journey, are a helpful example for us in our own lives and faith: like Reepicheep, many of us have been bounced this way and that by challenges. Reepicheep's single-minded devotion to Aslan drives him forward, though, despite obstacles and temptations. For Reepicheep, the *Dawn Treader* never seems to be moving toward his goal fast enough; he sits perched at the front of the ship, his gaze fixed on the eastern horizon. For most Christians, life's troubles are so great that the desires they once possessed for God's kingdom have been choked out or forgotten (see Christ's teaching on this in the parable of the sower in Matthew 13). While Christians shouldn't ignore or stop challenging injustice in this world, our motivation ought always be fixed on seeing God's kingdom come, as our Lord has taught us to pray (Luke 11:2–4). Like Reepicheep, we, too, ought to operate with single-minded devotion to Christ and his coming kingdom.

Some might challenge such a posture of single-minded devotion to the coming kingdom by saying it ignores the needs of our present world. Lewis, however, would contend that only by living for God's future reality can we rightly fight for truth in our world's present, broken reality: "If you read history you will find that the Christians who did most for the present world were just those who thought most of the next" (Chapter 10, Book 3, *Mere Christianity*).

By loving the next world, we won't love this world less. Instead, it is only by loving the present world through a steadfast devotion to Christ and his coming kingdom that we will ever love it *rightly*. Further, by fixing our gaze on God's in-breaking Kingdom, we will ensure that it is continually our destination. As the apostle Paul encouraged his readers in Colossae:

> If then you have been raised with Christ, seek the things that are above, where Christ is, seated at the right hand of God. Set your minds on things that are above, not on things that are on earth. For you have died, and your life is hidden with Christ in God. When Christ who is your life appears, then you also will appear with him in glory. (Col 3:1–4)

Or, as C. S. Lewis once told a group of young readers, the real-life equivalent of Reepicheep is "anyone in our world who devotes his whole life to seeking heaven" (*Letters to Children*, May 29, 1954). May we, like Reepicheep, do all we can to strive for God's kingdom in the present, pointing others toward him at every step along the way of this journey.

FOR REFLECTION

1 Eustace's transformation into a dragon, driven in large part by his own greed, and his later, painful transformation back into a boy paints a vivid picture of Christian conversion. What part of this story stood out most to you? How does this scene resonate with your own story of coming to Christian faith?

2 Reepicheep's bravery in *The Voyage of the Dawn Treader* is matched only by his devotion to reaching Aslan's country. Even when he faces obstacles, Reepicheep's gaze remains fixed on Aslan, making this chivalrous mouse a helpful model of a committed disciple. What obstacles are preventing you from embodying such devotion in your own life of faith?

THE SILVER CHAIR

O RIGINALLY TITLED *NIGHT UNDER NARNIA* BEFORE ITS release, *The Silver Chair* takes place only a few months after the story of *The Voyage of the Dawn Treader* in our time—but, of course, many years have passed in Narnia time.

SYNOPSIS & CHARACTERS

The only book in the Narnia Chronicles not to include any of the four Pevensie children, *The Silver Chair* begins with one new character to the Narnia series—Jill Pole—and one old—Eustace Scrubb, who is now a well-mannered, likeable boy. Jill and Eustace are called away from their dreadful school at the start of the story and into Narnia. There the great lion Aslan tasks them with finding Prince Rilian, Caspian's son and the heir to the throne. Though Caspian was still a young man in *The Voyage of the Dawn Treader*, some seventy years have since passed, and he is now an old man. Caspian's son, Prince Rilian, set out on a journey a decade earlier and has yet to return. He must be found in order that he take up his rightful seat as king of Narnia.

Before setting out on the journey, Eustace and Jill are given four signs to remember on their journey: they will meet an old friend; they must journey to the land of the giants in the north; they must follow the commands of the writing they find in stone; and they will be asked by Rilian to do something in Aslan's name. From there, Aslan breathes a great wind and sends them on their journey.

Very soon it becomes clear that they will not be able to remember and follow Aslan's signs. First, Eustace fails to recognize Caspian, as he has grown quite old since the last time they were together. Along the way of their journey, the two children meet Puddleglum the Marsh-wiggle. A tall, lanky character with oversized webbed feet and hands and a rather dreary disposition, Puddleglum possesses a level-headed, down-to-earth attitude that proves invaluable for the children's mission. As Professor Ash points out, Lewis modeled the character of Puddleglum after his gardener, Fred Paxford, who Lewis described as a pessimist on the outside but very much an optimist on the inside.

After barely avoiding being eaten by giants in the north during their autumn feast, the children find themselves with Puddleglum in Underland, which is ruled by the Lady of the Green Kirtle, a witch who captured Prince Rilian. With the help of Puddleglum, the children free not only themselves but also Rilian from the witch's capture. After she transforms into a giant snake, Rilian defeats the witch with a sword. The two children, Puddleglum, and Rilian return safely to Narnia. There they are able to see Caspian before his death and eventual resurrection by Aslan. The children return to their horrific school—joined briefly by Caspian, who helps Jill and Eustace against some bullies—and Rilian rules over Narnia as a beloved king.

BIBLICAL THEMES

While there are a variety of biblical themes scattered throughout the story of Jill and Eustace's adventures in *The Silver Chair*, we will discuss two here: Jill's encounter with Aslan, and Puddleglum's saving faith.

JILL ENCOUNTERS ASLAN

Not long after arriving in Narnia, Jill finds herself alone and very thirsty. When she hears what sounds like running water, she makes her way to the noise, only to find a clear, cool stream with a great lion lying beside it. Frozen by fear, Jill is torn between two great sensations: her incredible thirst and her fear of the lion.

When she is invited to drink, Jill confesses that she is "dying of thirst," but that she is also deathly afraid of what the lion might do if she comes any nearer. So Jill asks the lion series of questions about his intentions and whether he will harm her. It soon becomes clear that the lion is not going anywhere, that he will make no promise not to affect Jill, and that he has swallowed not only both girls and boys, but entire empires. Caught in this great dilemma, Jill's relentless thirst finally presses her forward to the water. When she takes a drink from the stream, the lion still watching over her, she realizes it is the "most refreshing water she had ever tasted" (Chapter 2).

After this dramatic introduction, Jill is told that she and Eustace would not have called out to Aslan had he not first been calling them—and it is then that Aslan reveals his task for the children.

What can Jill's first encounter with Aslan teach Christians about the Christian journey? First, one repeated theme in Lewis's Narnia Chronicles is that Aslan deserves the full respect and even fear his presence demands. From the Pevensie children's first hearing Aslan's name in *The Lion, the Witch and the Wardrobe*, they are warned that he is anything but safe. In this scene in *The Silver Chair*, it quickly becomes clear that Jill will not be unaffected by her encounter with Aslan. Similarly, we cannot approach Christ and expect to leave the encounter unchanged. Following Christ comes at a great cost. In following Christ, our desires no longer reflect our own lordship over our lives, but his. As such, our lives will necessarily look different after encountering Christ, which often means following a new direction for our lives or the same direction in a new way. But what is clear is that we will not meet Christ and remain unchanged. In this way, it is right to approach Christ with the gravity and weight he deserves. He is Lord of all (Eph 1:20–23; Col 1:13–19), and he desires all of who we are. Assuming anything less than this when we approach him would be a great mistake.

Second, as Jill realizes when she is frozen in fear of the lion, there is no other source to quench her thirst. *If drinking from this stream may cost me my life*, she must think, *then the most reasonable thing to do would be to find another stream*. But as Aslan makes clear to Jill, if it is full satisfaction for her thirst that she seeks, there is no other stream. Similarly, when Thomas asks Jesus how the disciples might know how to get to God the Father, Jesus replies: "I am the way, and the truth, and the life. No one comes to the Father except through me" (John 14:6). Though she had been on death's door, Jill's great thirst is quenched entirely as soon as she drinks from the stream beside Aslan. Likewise, for all those wrestling with similarly intense needs or desires, Jesus speaks: "I am the bread of life; whoever comes to me shall not hunger, and whoever believes in me shall never thirst" (John 6:35). When all of the crowds who had previously been following Jesus, captivated by his miracles, begin to leave in disappointment, Jesus turns to his remaining twelve disciples and asks what is perhaps one of the most human questions he ever spoke: "Do you want to go away as well?" (John 6:67). In response, it is unsurprisingly Simon Peter who eventually speaks up. "Lord, to whom shall we go? You have the words of eternal life" (John 6:68).

Even when others had left in disappointment, even as Jesus' words must have remained mysterious to all those who stayed, even as he considered the alternatives, Simon Peter acknowledged that there was simply no other option. Jesus—and Jesus alone—has the words to eternal life.

Following Jesus may cost us our life—or at least our life as we had previously envisioned it. But there is no other way to quench this universal thirst we all live with, apart from the one who says: "I am the living bread that came down from heaven. If anyone eats of this bread, he will live forever. And the bread that I will give for the life of the world is my flesh" (John 6:51).

PUDDLEGLUM'S SAVING FAITH

In another powerful scene from *The Silver Chair*, the children are on the verge of rescuing Prince Rilian when they are caught underground by the evil witch, the Lady of the Green Kirtle. Were it not for the saving, practical faith of Puddleglum, their mission may very well have failed.

In Chapter 12, "The Queen of the Underland," the Lady of the Green Kirtle doesn't respond to the children's attempt to free Rilian with a violent attack, but rather by throwing green powder on a fire and strumming an instrument akin to a mandolin. The music was so monotonous that "the less you noticed it, the more it got into your brain and your blood." Soon, the children find themselves under the spell of the evil Lady. All that they had previously believed to be real, they doubt to be anything more than a dream, as she speaks in a quiet, sweet tone.

There is no Narnia, the Lady of the Green Kirtle insists. Nor is there any place called England where the children go to school. There is no sun, and there is most certainly no Aslan. *This* is all there is, she insists: her Underland is the only real world. All that they speak of is only childish make-believe—ultimately, myth.

The children and Prince Rilian are on the verge of falling completely under the Witch's enchantment when Puddleglum musters all his strength, walks to the fire and stomps it out with his large, webbed Marsh-wiggle feet. With the fire out, the children and Prince can think more clearly, and Puddleglum replies to the Witch's lies with a practical voice of reason: "All I can say is that, in that case, the made-up things seem a good deal more important than the real ones. ... I'm on Aslan's side even if there isn't any Aslan to lead it" (Chapter 12). At this, the Lady of the Green Kirtle is revealed for who she truly is: a witch. She then assumes the form of a giant snake, and Prince Rilian finds the courage necessary to defeat her. Puddleglum's levelheaded reasoning and committed faith in the face of the Lady's sweet-spoken psychological games save the children and the prince when all hope of escaping her Underworld and returning to Narnia seemed lost.

What might this scene have to teach us about Christian growth? First, the Lady's demythologizing efforts, which she uses to enchant the children, Prince Rilian, and Puddleglum, are not so different from some attitudes toward Christianity today. While

Christians may not be called to question their faith in the reality of the sun, we are certainly asked to question our faith in the Son. *Did Jesus really believe that he was the Son of God?* we have likely been asked. *Did Jesus really die on the cross, and was he actually raised again on the third day? Isn't it silly to believe in God and heaven at all? Isn't it much more respectable to believe that this world is all there is? To believe in a world beyond the world that we can see and touch is childish, wishful thinking that any reasonable adult would outgrow, like any other children's story of their youth.*

It is in this same vein that the Lady of the Green Kirtle challenges the reality of Narnia and Aslan. The world around them, she claims, is all there is. And, as C. S. Lewis describes the enchanting music she's playing in the background, "the less you noticed it, the more it got into your brain and your blood." *Is there really a heaven? Is it not more reasonable to believe that this world is all there is? Is there even a God?*

In response to such claims, Puddleglum is offered as a portrait of clear-headed, committed faith. This practical-minded character responds by pointing out that, even if the realities that they know from experience *are* nothing more than their own imagination, then it's funny that they have been able to imagine something more important than the reality immediately around them. And this is an important point.

C. S. Lewis elaborates on this same point in "Is Theology Poetry?," a paper he presented to the Oxford Socratic Club. In this paper, Lewis notes that although one can make sense of the content of a dream while awake, the reverse is not true—and so "the waking world is judged more real because it can thus contain the dreaming world: the dreaming world is judged less real because it cannot contain the waking one." In both this paper and the scene of Puddleglum seeing through the witch's enchantment in the Underworld, Lewis is showing that any view of the world that says "what you see is all there is" cannot possibly hold all that we know to be true and real. The Christian worldview, unlike the narrow materialist worldview that suggests what is real is limited to visible realities, is broad enough to include not only all that science and reason posit as real, but much more, including the most important realities that cannot be perceived by sight.

As Puddleglum pointed out, it is silly to suggest that the most important realities are made up or childish. How odd it would be, Lewis is pointing out by way of Puddleglum, if children could dream up more important realities than what's offered by the "real world." But even if Narnia and Aslan are "made up," Puddleglum is going to continue following Aslan and living like a Narnian as long as he is able.

For Christians, the first takeaway from this story is to be encouraged: completely dismissing religious commitment results in a narrow view of the world, too narrow to possibly be true. Not only can Christianity allow for the findings of science, but it can also account for important realities that are beyond the reach of empirical study. The second lesson offered by Puddleglum's commitment to Aslan: Christians have the opportunity to witness to a reality different than that offered by secular culture. We can do this by remaining committed to following the living Son of God wherever he might lead and continuing to live as citizens of God's kingdom here and now. Giving thanks to God for all that we have, rather than assuming all we have is simply due to our own efforts, and loving others as God's beloveds, rather than seeing them as simply merely possessing value in so far as they can be of use to us—these are simple ways in which Christians are called to see the world differently, and in seeing the world differently, to be in the world differently. Such a commitment to God and his in-breaking kingdom will testify to the beauty, truth, and ultimate hope of Christianity in a hurting world that is dying for something to believe and hope in.

FOR REFLECTION

1   In the scene of Jill Pole's initial encounter with Aslan, she is struck by such fear that she nearly avoids the water streaming right in front of her, even as she's dying of thirst. When she asks if Aslan will promise not to do anything to her, he insists that he can't make such a promise. When she begins to wonder if there is another stream to quench her thirst, Aslan assures here there is not; this is the only stream. How does Jill's interaction with Aslan reflect on or change how you think about your relationship with Jesus?

2   Puddleglum serves as a model of committed, clear-head faith in the midst of worldviews that attempt to disorient us into denying what we know to be true. This otherwise pessimistic character gives the children the hope they need to defeat their captor and return to the land of Narnia by insisting that he intends to follow Aslan and live like a Narnian regardless

of whether the Lady of the Green Kirtle is correct. How might this scene help you respond to a purely rational, materialist view of the world that denies faith in God, Jesus' resurrection, and so many religious claims? Further, how might Puddleglum's clear-headed response in the face of the witch's enchantment and demythologizing efforts encourage you to remain committed to your Christian faith?

THE SPACE TRILOGY

DID YOU KNOW?

C. S. Lewis and his colleague and friend J. R. R. Tolkien agreed to each write a story exploring myth—Lewis, a space journey, and Tolkien, a time journey. While Lewis's first contribution, *Out of the Silent Planet*, was published in 1938, Tolkien's time journey remained only a fragment for many years. It was published posthumously by his son Christopher Tolkien in *The Lost Road and Other Writings* (1987).

C. S. Lewis first shared his space journey story with the Inklings, his group of literary friends in Oxford. On reading it in whole for the first time, J. R. R. Tolkien wrote: "I read this story in the original manuscript and was so enthralled that I could do nothing until I had finished it" (Letter to Stanley Unwin, March 2, 1938, *The Letters of J. R. R. Tolkien*).

In his preface to *That Hideous Strength*, C. S. Lewis notes that insofar as the book is "A Modern Fairy-Tale for Grown-Ups" (the book's subtitle), it shares a central idea with *The Abolition of Man*. Both books emphasize the objective values and natural laws that are a part of the fabric of reality, which children should be taught to recognize and which remain true even if they are denied by modern and postmodern philosophy.

As a young reader with a voracious appetite for books, C. S. Lewis's favorite authors included science fiction writers Jules Verne (*Around the World in Eighty Days* and *Twenty Thousand Leagues Under the Sea*) and H. G. Wells (*The Time Machine* and *The War of the Worlds*).

C. S. Lewis wrote his first piece of science fiction—a short story titled "To Mars and Back"—at age six.

The central protagonist in Lewis's Space Trilogy, Dr. Elwin Ransom (called "Ransom"), resembles J. R. R. Tolkien. Both are middle-aged (at the time of Lewis's writing); both are philologists; and both are professors at prestigious English universities, with this one important distinction: whereas Tolkien taught at Oxford, Ransom taught at Cambridge.

Lewis began but never finished a sequel to *Out of the Silent Planet* titled *The Dark Tower*. The book begins precisely where *Out of the Silent Planet* left off, and it deals with the themes of time and memory. Sixty-two pages of the unfinished manuscript were published in 1977.

SECTION ONE

INTRODUCING THE SPACE TRILOGY

I N THIS VIDEO EPISODE, PROFESSOR ASH INTRODUCES US TO C. S. Lewis's three books about space travel, most often referred to as the Space Trilogy: *Out of the Silent Planet* (1938), *Perelandra* (1943), and *That Hideous Strength* (1945). Just as he did in the Narnia Chronicles, in these stories Lewis allowed his imagination to dream up another world and ask, "What would it look like for God to show up here for the purpose of redemption?" In this section, we will go through a synopsis of each of these stories as well as overviewing their central characters.

SYNOPSIS & CHARACTERS

OUT OF THE SILENT PLANET

The first book in the Space Trilogy begins with Elwin Ransom, an unmarried philologist and professor from Cambridge University. Though he shares many similarities with his author, Lewis likely modeled the character of Ransom on his friend and fellow author, J. R. R. Tolkien. Ransom, who serves as the central protagonist in all three stories, is on a walking tour when he meets two men:

Professor Weston, an arrogant physicist with dreams of expanding humanity to the outer realms of the galaxy who serves as the story's central antagonist, and Dick Devine, a power-hungry politician who is driven by greed. Weston and Devine capture Ransom, and soon they are en route to Mars, called "Malacandra" in this story, aboard Weston's spaceship. On the journey, Ransom realizes the two men's evil interests and, upon arriving on Malacandra, he flees his captors and begins to explore the foreign world.

On Malacandra, Ransom meets a variety of alien beings, including the *hrossa*, slick-coated, rational creatures that can speak and spend their time fishing and creating poetry; *séroni*, 15-foot tall human like creatures with feather-covered bodies and who are the scholars of Malacandra; and *pfilfltriggi*, frog-like creatures who serve as miners and builders. It is one of the *hrossa*, a creature by the name of Hyoi, who befriends Ransom and teaches him not only the language but also their philosophy and way of life. Malacandra is also home to *Oyarsa* (plural Oyéresu), an *eldil* (angelic being) who rules the planet.

Ransom also is introduced to the history of Earth—referred to as Thulcandra, or "the silent planet," by those on Malacandra—and how its fall to evil led to its inhabitants being referred to as "bent." He is also told the story of the Bent One of the silent planet, who we might refer to as Satan, and how he was ultimately driven out and bound for his evil ways, and of Maleldil the Young, the Lord or Christ-figure of the story, who created and still rules over all things.

When Weston and Dick Devine catch up with Ransom, Weston fires his rifle and kills Ransom's new friend, Hyoi. It is then that they are ordered to leave Malacandra on their ship, returning to earth, where Professor C. S. Lewis, as a character, hears of and shares their story. Returned to earth, Ransom is tasked by Oyarsa with preventing Weston from any further evil.

PERELANDRA

Like the Narnia Chronicles, the floating-island world of Perelandra first came to Lewis as an image he could not shake until he was forced to write about it. The second story in Lewis's Space Trilogy, *Perelandra* tells the tale of Ransom's trip to Venus, or "Perelandra," in order to thwart the evil plans of the Bent One of Thulcandra (Satan).

Unlike our world, Perelandra is an Edenic planet that has never experienced evil or the fall. A world of magnificent natural beauty, Perelandra is made up of floating islands surrounded by golden sky and oceans. The planet's moving islands give Ransom the experience of being on a ship. He soon meets the Green Lady (whose name, we later learn, is Tinidril)—an unclothed, green-skinned woman who otherwise appears human and who is Perelandra's queen. Ransom is told about the planet's king and soon realizes that these two are the only two "humans" on Perelandra; they represent the unfallen Adam and Eve of Earth. In their unfallen state, the king and queen enjoy direct communion with Maleldil, the Christ-figure of the Space Trilogy. Further, Ransom learns that the two have been commanded not to spend the night on the Fixed Land, the only nonfloating, nonmoving spot on Perelandra.

Interrupting the scene, Professor Weston arrives in the story, proclaiming his reformed ways, but he is soon overtaken by a demonic power and attempts to persuade the Green Lady to stay overnight on the Fixed Land—the one thing she has been commanded *not* to do. It soon becomes clear that Weston is no longer the man he once was, but is now referred to as the "Un-man," the embodiment of the Bent One from Earth. With an upside-down logic that twists everything Ransom and the Green Lady say, Weston continues to try to persuade the queen of Perelandra to defy Maleldil's command.

Ransom is soon chasing Weston across the sea to the Fixed Land, using both psychological and physical force to stop his evil plans. When Weston is finally defeated—but not before Ransom's heel is deeply wounded—Ransom celebrates with the king and queen of Perelandra, joined also by the Oyéresu of Malacandra and Perelandra, for preventing the second fall. The book ends with Ransom returning to earth, vowing to prevent the spread of evil on his own planet.

THAT HIDEOUS STRENGTH: A MODERN FAIRY-TALE FOR GROWN-UPS

Unlike the other two stories in C. S. Lewis's Space Trilogy, the third book in the series takes place not on Mars, Venus, or another alien planet, but on Earth. *That Hideous Strength* is unique in another way as well: rather than focusing primarily on Ransom, the two central characters of this story are a scholarly, newlywed couple by the name of Mark and Jane Studdock. The story follows the couple and their distinct roles in response to the N.I.C.E. (National Institute for Co-ordinated Experiments), a scientific agency whose efforts for "progress" are unveiled to be not only sinister but even supernatural in nature.

The story opens with two central characters: Mark Studdock, a sociologist hungry to gain access to the "inner ring" of his university's academic circles, and his wife Jane, a PhD candidate at the same university who is writing her dissertation on John Donne but who has currently lost interest in her subject and so spends her time as a housewife.

The book begins with Jane remembering a nightmare she had the night before. In it, a prisoner named Alcasan was being sentenced to death. She is disturbed to find, that morning, the same man's face on the front page of the newspaper with the headline: "Execution of Alcasan: Scientist Bluebeard Goes to Guillotine." The story then turns to her husband, Mark, who is invited to meet Lord Feverstone—Dick Devine from *Out of the Silent Planet*, and Weston's partner in crime—which leads to Mark being invited to apply to join the N.I.C.E. Quickly, the N.I.C.E.'s scientific work and ultimate aims are revealed as eliminating the weak for the sake of the strong (Chapter 2). Even after hearing such despicable plans, Mark is thrilled by the prospect of upward mobility—financially, socially, and professionally.

Returning to Jane, she realizes that her dreams are not only continuing, but are actually reflecting reality—she has the gift of premonition. Soon the two are set on very different paths: Mark on the side of the N.I.C.E. and its vision of human progress— dominating the weak for the sake of the powerful—and Jane on the side of a group who live in the nearby town of St. Anne's. The head of the N.I.C.E. is revealed to be the severed head of the scientist Alcasan—who had appeared in Jane's nightmare at the start of the book; who is kept alive by blood transfusions; and who is in touch with demonic, spiritual powers—while the head of the St. Anne's group is Ransom, the protagonist from *Out of the Silent Planet* and *Perelandra* and the rightful heir of King Arthur. It soon becomes clear that this is nothing short of a battle between the forces of good and evil on Earth.

Mark is given work as a writer for the propaganda newspaper of the N.I.C.E., while Jane is soon taken captive by the same organization, which hopes to take advantage of her revealed psychic abilities. Further, it's revealed that the N.I.C.E. has plans to dig up the body of Merlin and recruit his magical powers for its own evil intentions. Waking before his capture, Merlin finds his way to the community at St. Anne's and joins their efforts against the N.I.C.E. Mark is saved by Merlin's defeat of the N.I.C.E., allowing him to rejoin his now-rescued wife and the community at St. Anne's. Upon completing his task of preventing Earth's conquest by the evil forces at work in the N.I.C.E., Ransom is flown to Perelandra to be finally and fully healed of his wound from the Un-man.

FOR REFLECTION

1 Like the Chronicles of Narnia, Lewis's Space Trilogy seem out of place when compared to his other writings. Why did Lewis write *Out of the Silent Planet*, *Perelandra*, and *That Hideous Strength*?

2 Does Lewis's purpose for writing his Space Trilogy make the series still relevant today? If so, how might it apply to our current situation?

SECTION TWO

A CLOSER LOOK AT *PERELANDRA*

N OW THAT WE HAVE TAKEN A BIRD'S-EYE OVERVIEW OF EACH
book in Lewis's Space Trilogy, we will take a closer look at
three important themes in the second book, *Perelandra*. These
themes parallel not only biblical texts, but also our lives as
Christ's disciples.

BIBLICAL THEMES

A HEAVENLY ENCOUNTER

Professor Ash breaks up his study of *Perelandra* into three sec-
tions. This story begins not with the Space Trilogy's protagonist,
Ransom, but with C. S. Lewis, who is also a character in the book.
The first section of our study of *Perelandra* involves C. S. Lewis's
arriving at Ransom's cottage and meeting an angelic being there.
A heavenly encounter is the first biblical theme we will consider.

In Lewis's Space Trilogy, the angelic, heavenly creatures are not
called angels, but "eldil" (plural "eldila"). While we might typically
think of angels—if we think of angels at all—as bringing warmth,
joy, and overall pleasant feelings, the first experience Lewis has

of this eldil is "very unpleasant." It gives off an incredible, consistent light, which strikes Lewis's eyes. Lewis finds himself confused, unable to categorize this creature—animate or inanimate both seem inadequate to describe this eldil. Perhaps most interestingly, Lewis finds himself afraid, but in a way he has never before experienced fear. He is confident that the eldil is what we would call "good," but he is surprised to find himself drawn not to it, but suddenly wanting to flee. Lewis realizes that his taste for "goodness" may not be what he had previously thought (Chapter 1).

Not unlike biblical accounts of human-angelic encounters, Lewis's meeting with the eldil in Ransom's cottage is described largely in terms of fear. "Do not be afraid" is one of the first things Gabriel says to Mary when he appears to share the news of her pregnancy (Luke 1:30). "Fear not" are the first words the angels speak to the shepherds when they appear to share the good news of Jesus' birth (Luke 2:10). And when the women come to Jesus' tomb and find it empty, the angels' first words of explanation are "do not be afraid" (Matt 28:5). Clearly fear is an appropriate—though perhaps surprising—response to an encounter with an angel. This fear is not merely in response to the angelic being's alien appearance, but to something much deeper.

Lewis, both as author as well as character in his own story, puts his finger on the confusion of this experience: "As long as what you are afraid of is something evil, you may still hope that the good may come to your rescue. But suppose you struggle through to the good and find that is also dreadful?" (Chapter 1). Part of Lewis's fear, it seems, is in response to his own utter inadequacy in the face of this angelic goodness. Rather than celebrating this holy presence—as we might imagine our first response would be—our actual response is more likely to be shame. When we are brought face-to-face with the holy goodness of heaven, our most immediate response will surely be to recognize that we do not fit in as we are. This, it seems, is a sign not of spiritual immaturity, but of maturity. Early on in Jesus' teaching ministry, Peter glimpses a hint of Jesus' true identity, and his response, quoting Isaiah, is striking: "Depart from me, for I am a sinful man, O Lord" (Luke 5:8). When the reality of heaven shows up in human form, it is not, first and foremost, a comfort, but a discomforting goodness that reveals our own fallenness.

This right recognition of the goodness of heaven, and our own distance from it, reveals our need for help. If we are to enter into the holy presence of God, we will need a mediator—it is not a journey we can make on our own, or which we would even desire if we saw it firsthand. But recognizing this infinite chasm between what we will be and what we are now is the first step in moving toward that end toward which God is leading us, which is nothing short of himself.

EXPERIENCING GOD'S PERFECT CREATION

The second section of *Perelandra* involves Ransom's landing and initial experience on the alien planet Perelandra. As Professor Ash notes in the video, Ransom has a number of experiences that reveal he has never been anywhere quite like this. Perelandra is unique to all human experiences in that it is unfallen—it is precisely how God first intended creation to be, in right relation both to humans and to himself. What might it be like for a fallen human to experience God's perfect creation? That is precisely the question and theme we will now explore.

Perelandra's perfection is first revealed to Ransom through his sense of taste. Though he had not even been aware of his thirst, at his first drink of Perelandra's water, Ransom realizes he has never tasted anything so delicious, so satisfying as this. When he has his first taste of the yellow, globe-shaped fruit that grows from trees on Perelandra, Ransom finds himself not merely tasting a new taste but having a new kind of experience altogether (Chapter 3). Ransom's first inclination is to reach out for another taste of the fruit, but he finds he is no longer hungry nor thirsty, and he thinks to himself that to repeat such an incredible pleasure would be rude or greedy. He also finds himself in awe of the fact that, even though his first experience upon Perelandra's water-covered surface was spent swimming through massive waves, he is not tired in the least from his efforts.

Looking upon his new surroundings, with a golden sky overhead and an emerald sea that stretches in high-cresting waves as far as he can see, Ransom is struck by the unspeakable beauty of this planet. In trying to take it all in, Ransom quickly realizes is that language itself is insufficient—such beauty is beyond words. The sum of Ransom's first experiences on this foreign planet is described by the phrase "excessive pleasure." For the first time in his life, Ransom is struck by his freedom from any sense of guilt. It is an altogether alien experience.

When Ransom has his first experience with another human— the Green Lady, the queen of Perelandra, a goddess-like creature who appears as though she's been carved out of green stone—they exchange a series of curious experiences that reveal just how foreign both are to one another. Although both are unclothed, Ransom realizes he is free of either desire for her or shame at his own nakedness. Their nakedness simply *is*. Ransom is also struck by an unparalleled calmness in the Green Lady. Unlike every other human he has met before, the Green Lady expresses no sense of resignation or exhaustion with the way things are. She is genuinely and completely at peace.

By contrast, the Green Lady is confused by Ransom's first words: "I come in peace."

"What is 'peace'?" she asks in response. Having never experienced anything other than peace, the Green Lady has no way to understand Ransom's greeting. How would one know what's meant by the serenity of peace without experiencing conflict? Further, she is struck by Ransom's sense of himself, and his awareness of his place in time. To think of oneself in this way is as foreign to the Green Lady as her calmness is to Ransom.

But most unique of all their differences is the Green Lady's relation to Maleldil—the Christian God, incarnate on Earth as Jesus. Unlike humanity's shattered relationship with God at the fall, the queen of Perelandra enjoys direct, unmediated communion with Maleldil. Revelation is not something that is passed down to her; she is presently communing with God.

While Ransom is pressed into a sitting position by a great weight at that moment, he is also overwhelmed by a state of pure bliss. The Green Lady, in contrast, receives from Maleldil a vision of other worlds. Soon, Maleldil reveals to the Green Lady that he once became incarnate on Ransom's planet, a revelation that she had not previously known and which takes Ransom by surprise. Maleldil's revelation to the Green Lady is both present and unmediated—completely foreign to fallen humanity's experience, but precisely as we were created to enjoy.

These first experiences of Ransom's landing on Perelandra recall the picture of unfallen creation from the first chapters of Genesis, when humanity lived at peace with creation, completely satisfied with God's provisions and in direct communion with its creator. Though difficult to imagine on this side of the fall, Lewis's description of Perelandra invites us to imagine what it would be like to live as God first created us—and the ultimate reunion toward which Christ is calling and leading us (2 Cor 5:18).

WESTON, TEMPTATION, AND THE PROGRESSION OF EVIL

The third section of *Perelandra* that Professor Ash discusses concerns Weston's arrival on Perelandra, thirsty to conquer other planets and spread his newfound "spirituality"; his becoming the "Un-man" after calling evil into his own body; and the temptation he brings to this unfallen planet. While the Green Lady previously was sure of Maleldil's teaching on what she should and should not do, with Weston's arrival, all is questioned. This portrait of temptation helps illumine how we, too, can be led astray from what we know to be God's will for our lives.

The first way that Weston, now called the Un-man, tries to tempt the Green Lady is by questioning Maleldil's commandment that, while she is permitted to visit the lone Fixed Land on this planet of floating islands, she must never spend the night (Chapter 8). The Un-man's temptation begins by suggesting that surely it is okay for her to at least *think* about it. The Un-man describes this imaginative practice as wisdom, and he falsely offers stories and poetry as an example of such wisdom. Fortunately, the Green Lady is not convinced that imagining something that is clearly commanded not to act on is wise.

The Un-man goes on to suggest that by disobeying Maleldil she will become more wise, more beautiful, and whole, like the women of his world. At this suggestion, the Green Lady begins to imagine herself becoming not only more who Maleldil created her to be, but as the angelic eldila are (Chapter 8). The Un-man's relentless tempting continues in the next chapter, where he promises that the queen's disobedience will result in the kind of wisdom and beauty that not only matches but surpasses the women of Earth. When Ransom tires to break into the conversation and reveal the Un-man's lies, he realizes she has no way to understand deceit. The Un-man takes the opportunity to insist that Ransom doesn't want her to become wise, that he wants her to remain ignorant of the things the Un-man offers.

In the Un-man's temptation of the Green Lady, we see a similar kind of upside-down logic as we see in *The Screwtape Letters* as well as in the serpent in the garden (Gen 3:1-7). While Ransom's first words were of peace, the Un-man insists that Ransom is actually the one who is to be feared (Chapter 9). Even when the Un-man admits his true intentions—to bring "Death in abundance"—he presents his evil in an upside-down way so that the Green Lady will begin to desire precisely that which will do her ill. Soon, she is being led to believe that to trust in and wait on Maleldil is a kind of disobedience. Under the Un-man's guidance, obedience has become disobedience; light has become darkness, and darkness, light. Thus is the upside-down nature of sin's captivating logic.

At this point, it is worth emphasizing two points concerning temptation in our own lives, brought to light by the Un-man's efforts to tempt the Green Lady away from Maleldil. The first thing to note is that evil does not arrive in Perelandra with any great temptation; it appears subtly at first. The Un-man first tries to lead the Green Lady away from Maleldil not by inviting her to *do* anything, but simply to *think* of what it might be like to disobey. Of course, once she has *thought* of disobeying Maleldil, the Un-man is able to begin to persuade her that disobedience might actually be that which she should do. But it all begins with something small: the suggestion to imagine something she knows she should not do.

This progression of temptation from something very small to something great is very often true of our own experience of temptation. One is less likely to be tempted to walk away from God by a great temptation than by some small temptation, or by a slow, steady series of temptations. As Lewis warns us in *The Screwtape Letters*, "The safest road to hell is the gradual one" (Letter 12).

Second, we learn that temptation begins not with a call to action, but with an idea. As James writes, this is precisely how sin often starts: "Each person is tempted when he is lured and enticed by his own desire. Then desire when it has conceived gives birth to sin, and sin when it is fully grown brings forth death" (Jas 1:14–15). The sting of sin does not begin with death—even though that is its natural end. Instead, it often begins with an evil thought or with desire led astray.

In his Sermon on the Mount, Jesus addresses a number of commandments, drawing his listeners to even stricter standards than what they were used to. On the topic of the physical act of adultery, which those listening would have known to be a violation of God's command, Jesus teaches that if we do not guard against wayward glances or lustful thoughts, then we have already committed adultery inwardly (Matt 5:27–28). Adultery, as with many temptations and sins, often begins not with an evil act, but with an evil thought.

For the Christian, not only our physical actions but our imagination and thoughts are of importance. What begins as a simple thought can grow into an unimaginable lifestyle, far from God's wishes for his beloved creation. It is for this reason that the apostle Paul wrote to the early church to "take every thought captive" (2 Cor 10:5) and to encourage those early disciples to guard their thoughts:

> Whatever is true, whatever is honorable, whatever is just, whatever is pure, whatever is lovely, whatever is commendable, if there is any excellence, if there is anything worthy of praise, think about these things. What you have learned and received and heard and seen in me—practice these things, and the God of peace will be with you. (Phil 4:8-9)

By encouraging his readers to keep their hearts and minds on the good, the true, and the beautiful, Paul underlines that our imaginations shape our actions. To avoid being tempted to fall away from the Lord, our imaginations must be shaped by that which honors God—and in being so shaped, renewed, as Paul put it to the early church in Rome: "Do not be conformed to this world, but be transformed by the renewal of your mind, that by testing you may discern what is the will of God, what is good and acceptable and perfect" (Rom 12:2).

By taking great care to consider the different voices that attempt to shape our imaginations, we will be better prepared to say "no" to those voices that seek to lead us astray, often ever so subtly, sometimes even disguising themselves as good, and to be better able to say "yes" to the Lord's voice, which still calls out, "Follow me."

FOR REFLECTION

1 How does C. S. Lewis's description of his imaginary encounter with an eldil in Ransom's cottage compare to other depictions of humans meeting angels that you've seen in popular movies, books, or TV shows? Why do you think such depictions of human-angelic encounters look different than this? What might we have to learn from this scene in *Perelandra*?

2 With Ransom's first experience of Perelandra in mind, read Genesis 1:26–2:25 with your group. What similarities do you notice? What differences? What excites you most about this account? What challenges you? How does this description of unfallen creation in Perelandra and the first part of Genesis compare to the description of reconciled creation in Revelation 21–22?

3   The Un-man's temptation of the Green Lady has many parallels to the biblical scene of humanity's temptation in the garden. Read aloud the account of the serpent's temptation in Genesis 3:1–7 and discuss with your group the similarities to the Green Lady's temptation in *Perelandra*. In what ways do the serpent's lies mirror the Un-man's? In what ways do they differ? How does Eve's response to the serpent compare to the Green Lady's response to the Un-man? How might this study of temptation help us see through temptations in our own lives?

A GRIEF OBSERVED AND "THE WEIGHT OF GLORY"

A GRIEF OBSERVED

DID YOU KNOW?

C. S. Lewis was nearly 60 years old when he married (Helen) Joy Davidman, first at the Oxford Registry Office in April of 1956, then again in the hospital on March 21, 1957.

A Grief Observed (1961) was originally published under the pseudonym N. W. Clerk. A number of readers sent copies of the book to C. S. Lewis, not knowing he had written it himself. It wasn't until the year after his own death that Lewis's real name replaced the pseudonym.

Throughout the book, Lewis refers to his deceased beloved as "H." Though she went by Joy, Lewis's wife's first name was Helen.

INTRODUCING *A GRIEF OBSERVED*

In the first half of this video, we will reflect with Professor Ash on what is perhaps C. S. Lewis's most personal book: *A Grief Observed*

(1961). Shortly after losing his wife to bone cancer on July 13, 1960, Lewis began writing down his reflections on his grief. Though these reflections were not meant for the public, by September, Lewis showed a friend the writing, and they were discussing the possibility of publication. The collection was published the following year under the pseudonym N. W. Clerk.

While *A Grief Observed* is not as clearly structured as the rest of Lewis's writing, it is divided into four chapters. In his discussion of this work, Professor Ash focuses on two aspects of the book: Lewis's personal experience of grief and his reflections on God.

THE EXPERIENCE OF GRIEF

Part of the lasting value of *A Grief Observed* is that, in his trademark lucid writing style, C. S. Lewis candidly captures what the experience of grief feels like. Like a man narrating his own surgery, the book's account of grief is painful in its honest reflections—but this is what has made it such a literary gift. Few authors have done so well at capturing the universal experience of death—and the corresponding confusing feelings of grief—as Lewis.

Whether you're going through grief yourself or have a loved one who is and are unsure how to help, *A Grief Observed* can be a real help. As Professor Ash suggests, it's not a bad idea to have several copies of the book on hand to give to those suffering the loss of a loved one.

What does grief feel like? While each experience of grief is unique, there are some universal themes. Lewis offers a vivid portrait of his own experience, providing a helpful insight into what can be a complex, confusing time.

FEAR

"No one ever told me that grief feels so much like fear," Lewis writes in the first sentence of *A Grief Observed*. Lewis was no stranger to grief—he had lost his own mother to cancer before his tenth birthday—but this was a new kind of grief, the grief of a spouse, with strange new flavors that Lewis describes as echoing fear.

Lewis refers to his own restlessness, his unsettled stomach, and his yawning. Later, he admits that his grief still feels like fear, this time adding that it's a bit like suspense (Chapter 3). Whereas before Joy's death he felt as though he never had enough time, now, it seems like time is all he has, and yet he can never relax. Lewis compares his experience of grief to fear to show the way in which both emotions prevent us from being at ease. Grief, like fear, is unsettling; there is no "coming down," or at least, not for long. Grief is, as Lewis later notes, not finally a state but a process (Chapter 4).

LAZINESS

While Lewis confesses that he is able to attend to his own work much as usual, he also admits that he largely lacks the effort to do the simplest of things: shaving, or reading a letter. Part of the reason for this laziness is the seeming pointlessness of such mundane activities in the face of such devastating loss. Grief takes a great amount of emotional energy, but it can also appear in the form of physical exhaustion. His description of the feelings of utter exhaustion that accompany grief can help us sympathize with a loved one who simply does not have the energy to do the most basic of normal tasks.

GUILT

Another feeling that Lewis associates with his grief is guilt. Speaking of the ebb and flow of his grief, Lewis notes that when he actually begins to find a break in the overwhelming weight of his grief, his reprieve is often cut short by guilt pains. This guilt comes in the form of feeling bad for feeling better, as though it were not quite right for him to be feeling better just yet (Chapter 3). Like Lewis in the early wake of his loss, there is very little reprieve for those experiencing grief. Even the brief glimmers of release can have a guilt-tinged shadow.

SEPARATED FROM THE WORLD

Another way Lewis describes his grief is that it's like having a concussion: not only is the mind dazed, but suddenly it is as though there is an "invisible blanket between the world and me" (Chapter 1).

In addition to being an unsettling feeling, grief can also be incredibly isolating. In a way that few other experiences do, grief seems to mark us off from others. Lewis remarks on the experience of walking down the street and noticing someone who knows of his loss walking toward him, trying to decide whether to mention his loss or not. Lewis refers to the experience as feeling as though he is now an embarrassment to everyone he knows—some of whom avoid him to avoid the embarrassment.

While the rest of the world goes on largely as it always has, those in grief remain painfully aware of their loss and, suddenly, their own exclusion from the normal course of life. This feeling of isolation can make grief a self-centered experience, which underlines the need for community—even when those suffering grief are pained by both the presence and the absence of others. A friend who is willing to take the time not to try to cure or fix the grief, but simply to sit with one who is experiencing this isolating loss, can be a lifesaving gift. It is the kind of love that says, sometimes with words, sometimes only with a look, that although your friend feels—and perhaps in many ways is—completely alone, you're there for your friend.

WHERE IS GOD?

In addition to reflecting on his own emotional experience of grief, much of C. S. Lewis's observations in *A Grief Observed* concern his relationship not with "H.," but with God. These reflections take up the majority of this book's theme, and the majority of these writings reveal C. S. Lewis the famed Christian apologist in his most open, honest struggles with doubt. Some have suggested that Lewis lost his faith in God at the end of his life, but that would be an incomplete picture of his experience. In order to respond to such a claim, one must account for his reflections as a whole collection.

Is God Absent?

Lewis begins writing about his experience of God—or lack thereof—following the death of his wife by questioning the seeming sudden and complete silence of God: "It's easy enough to say that God seems absent at our greatest need because He is absent—non-existent. But then why does He seem so present when, to put it quite frankly, we don't ask for Him?"

Though some of Lewis's frustration with God is due to his loss itself, it's also partly due to the confusing divine silence. Why,

Lewis asks, does God seem so near when times are good, but scarce when we really need him? It is a painfully honest question without easy answers, but it is worth asking nonetheless. Elsewhere, he compares his experience to that of knocking on God's door and hearing the door lock from the inside and footsteps in retreat. This feeling of being completely abandoned by God is, as Professor Ash notes, a low point in Lewis's experience. Fortunately, it does not last.

Is God Good?

In Chapter 2, Lewis begins to wonder whether, even if God is not absent, if he is a God we can actually go to for comfort. Is this God really *good*? Or, as Professor Ash notes, is this God instead a "Cosmic Sadist" who takes pleasure in our suffering? It seems an almost unimaginable question for C. S. Lewis, the great defender of the Christian faith, to ask. And yet, mired in his grief, he does. What does Lewis mean by this claim, and how could he make it?

Let's take a moment to remind ourselves of the details of Lewis's relationship with Joy: When the couple were married in the Oxford hospital on March 21, 1957, with Joy on what they thought was her deathbed, they were not expecting a remission from cancer and years of happy married life together at the Kilns— and yet that's exactly what they received. Eventually Joy's bone cancer returned, and, in July of 1960, Lewis was left feeling alone, confused, and hurt. And so Lewis begins to ask whether God might actually find pleasure in his pain.

Fortunately, again, it doesn't last. Lewis realizes that this picture of a God who delights in human suffering is too anthropomorphic—describing God according to human characteristics—to be helpful. He admits that such thoughts were only in anger, an attempt to make himself feel better (Chapter 3). Nor, Lewis concedes, can he conclude that God is evil, even if he struggles to properly understand God's goodness at such deeply painful times.

DOES GOD HURT TO HEAL?

In Chapter 3, Lewis admits that he no longer feels the door to God is closed and locked. And yet, he still feels the wounds of his loss deeply. It is this tension that leads Lewis to suggest that either these deep pains he is experiencing are unnecessary—and thus there is either no God or an evil one—or else they are necessary, and will turn out, somehow, for his own good. Lewis determines that God must be compared to that of a good surgeon: God's cutting hurts, undeniably, but the cuts are there not for the purpose of his pain and suffering, but for healing—even when he cannot yet see how.

Here, Lewis concludes that even if he were to ask God to relent, if this pain will somehow mean his or his loved one's good, then "if he stopped before the operation was complete, all the pain up to that point would have been useless" (Chapter 3).

IS IT BEST TO PRAISE GOD?

Were someone to stop short of finishing *A Grief Observed*, they might get the idea that losing his wife to cancer left a blow on C. S. Lewis's faith from which he was unable to recover. But that would be an incomplete picture of the story. In reality, Lewis concludes his reflections on his grief not in disbelief at all, but claiming that praise is now his proper response: as H. was a gift from God, "by praising [God] I can still, in some degree, enjoy her, and already, in some degree, enjoy Him" (Chapter 4).

Lewis admits that any understanding of God as merely a means to our lost loved ones is in reality no idea of God at all, but of something else. For God can never be a means to an end, but only ever our true, final, and full end—our ultimate good. This picture of God as our true and final purpose recalls the final scene in the Bible, where God comes down to make his home among us, wiping away every tear in the process:

> Behold, the dwelling place of God is with man. He will dwell with them, and they will be his people, and God himself will be with them as their God. He will wipe away every tear from their eyes, and death shall be no more, neither shall there be mourning, nor crying, nor pain anymore, for the former things have passed away. (Rev 21:3–4)

It is only by knowing that this portrait of God wiping away all of his children's tears is the end of our story that we can be encouraged, even in the midst of our deepest pain, to live lives of praise. It is only by being reminded, ever so gently, of the end of our story that we can be strengthened to mourn not as those without hope, but as those with hope unending (1 Thess 4:13).

As Professor Ash notes, Lewis concludes this account of his grief and his progression through feeling God's absence, evil, and finally worthiness of praise by suggesting he has no practical problem before him. He knows what he has been called to do, and so he must act on it: "I know the two great commandments [Love God, love your neighbor], and I'd better get on with them" (Chapter 4).

FOR REFLECTION

1   C. S. Lewis describes a variety of emotions he experienced after losing his wife, Joy, to bone cancer. Which of these experiences were you most able to relate with, either out of your own experiences of grief or in others'? Which of these emotions did you find surprising?

2   In *A Grief Observed*, Lewis expresses great doubt in and even anger toward God. However, why would it be inaccurate to say Joy's death resulted in Lewis losing his Christian faith?

3   In his reflections on his relationship with God throughout his process of grief, Lewis experiences distance, anger, and, finally, praise for God. How might Lewis provide a helpful model for those of us wrestling with grief after losing a loved one?

"THE WEIGHT OF GLORY"

DID YOU KNOW?

Lewis delivered this famous sermon from the University Church of St. Mary the Virgin on June 8, 1941. First built in the thirteenth century, the church has been the site of many historical events, including the trial of the Oxford martyrs for refusing to recant their Protestant beliefs in the 1550s and sermons delivered by John Wesley, Oxford student and founder of Methodism, in the 1740s.

One of those in the audience when C. S. Lewis delivered this sermon was his gardener, Fred Paxford. After hearing "The Weight of Glory" delivered, Paxford declared that Lewis had missed his calling—he believed Lewis should have been a preacher!

C. S. Lewis delivered "The Weight of Glory" two years into World War II, nearly four years from its end.

INTRODUCING "THE WEIGHT OF GLORY"

In what many call Lewis's most famous sermon, "The Weight of Glory," Lewis expounds on the mystery of heaven and what this reality means for our day-to-day lives. It's worth noting that the historical context for Lewis's message: he preached this sermon on June 8, 1941, from the pulpit of Oxford's University Church of St. Mary the Virgin. He was in a war-torn country, two years into World War II. The church congregation surely could not have helped but think of eternity while their nation's capital was being bombed. What, then, do Christians look forward to when Scripture speaks of the glory of our future with God? That is the question to which Lewis responds in this powerful sermon, and he notes five promises of Scripture concerning our heavenly state: "firstly, that we shall be with Christ; secondly, that we shall be like Him; thirdly, ... we shall have 'glory'; fourthly, that we shall, in some sense, be fed or feasted or entertained; and, finally, that we shall have some sort of official position in the universe."

WHAT OF OUR GLORY?

After noting these five promises of Scripture concerning our future state with God, C. S. Lewis focuses his attention on the promise of our glory. In so doing, he confesses that the word "glory" brings about two equally confusing ideas: fame and luminosity. What are we to make of such ideas as they relate to our future with God? That is the question toward which we will now turn.

FAME

As fame generally means being more popularly known than other people, C. S. Lewis notes that fame is, in many ways, a competitive passion. It is for this reason that interpreting Scripture's promise of our future glory with God in terms of fame is so troubling to Lewis. In the many decades that have passed since C. S. Lewis first delivered this sermon, the explosion of technological advancements and proliferation of electronic media have made the reality of fame as a competitive passion more tempting than Lewis could have possibly imagined. Today, the desire to be famous not for doing anything particularly remarkable or meaningful, but simply to be famous for the sake of fame, is a very real temptation for many. Of course, that hardly seems to be the kind of "glory" God desires for us. What, then, are we to make of such a promise?

Lewis reminds us that great Christian thinkers throughout history have thought of Scripture's promise of our glory with God as somehow concerning our fame or recognition—but with one key difference. Rather than understanding our heavenly fame as coming from others, this fame is to come from none other than God, the creator of all. It's the response we find in Jesus' parable of the talents: "Well done, good and faithful servant," Jesus will say like the master in the parable, welcoming the faithful servant, "You have been faithful over a little; I will set you over much. Enter into the joy of your master" (Matt 25:21). This is what we should all long to hear at the end of our days.

It is not, then, that our desire to be admired or revered is wrong, but that it has been turned away from its rightful audience. While the secular vision of fame and celebrity is alive and well, proliferated by magazines and TV shows that offer the promise of our glory before an ever-present audience of human faces, the biblical vision of God-granted fame that receives and welcomes us as God's beloved is the rightful aim of our life. While the praise of man is fickle, changing just as quickly as the seasons, being embraced by God's unending delight in us should rightly be our ultimate hope for our lives. And this is, Lewis notes, a proper understanding of what the Bible speaks of in terms of our future glory.

Like an animal being praised by its owner for its obedience or like a child praised by its loving parents for a job well done, we hope that, at the end of our days, we will be received by the One who can finally and fully satisfy our life-long need to be acknowledged; loved by the One who knows us better than we know ourselves; and welcomed by the God who delights in us.

LUMINOSITY

The second idea C. S. Lewis addresses concerning our future glory in God's ultimate presence is that of luminosity. It is a peculiar idea, Lewis admits, for who would desire to be a giant light bulb for all of eternity? Of course, this question misses the point. The idea of glory as luminosity has to do with beauty, the kind of beauty that is beyond words. This sort of unspeakable beauty is so rare that we are fortunate if we manage to experience it once or twice in a lifetime, and we spend the rest of our lives yearning to return to that moment.

Here Lewis comes to an idea that runs like a thread throughout his work: the idea of joy experienced most greatly as longing. Expressed most poignantly in *Surprised by Joy*, which we discussed in Episode 4, Lewis uses the German word *Sehnsucht* to express this deep yearning to get back to the fleeting moments of indescribable joy that we remember for a lifetime. Of course, as he notes in the present sermon, even if we were able to return to those moments, we would find not the beauty we had longed for, but an empty idol: the beautiful objects or experiences "are good images of what we really desire; but if they are mistaken for the thing itself they turn into dumb idols" ("The Weight of Glory").

Such beauty, Lewis notes, points always beyond itself, to a future, unending joy, leaving us with a deep yearning that will remain unquenched on this side of eternity. Such yearning, of course, is not unique to Christians; it is part of what it means to be human. "The Kingdom of God is what we all of us hunger for above all other things even when we don't know its name or realize that it's what we're starving to death for," writes Frederick Buechner. "The Kingdom of God is where we belong. It is home, and whether we realize it or not, I think we are all of us homesick for it"[1]

On this idea of heavenly glory as luminosity, Lewis goes on to note a curious desire that he suggests arises in each one of us who are fortunate enough to experience such remarkable beauty. What is curious is that it is not enough merely to be a witness of such beauty—we want to be drawn into it. Indeed, our greatest desire, Lewis suggests, is to be united with this unspeakable beauty that points us toward the holiness and goodness of God. And we are promised that, one day, by God's grace, we will be. Our heavenly glory, as Lewis makes clear, will not be a bodiless, ghostlike experience of somber worship, as some church services might mislead us to believe. Instead, our communion with God will be joy in the fullest, overflowing sense. Our future glory will be the kind of union with beauty that our most sensual moments of unspeakable delight only point toward.

GOD'S GLORY IN OUR NEIGHBOR

Before he concludes this sermon, C. S. Lewis reminds his audience that we will continue to experience grief and straining even as we long for our true homecoming. But even as we wait for God's full communion with creation, we are reminded that it is our duty, as Christ's disciples, to reveal to others that they are so much more than a "mere mortal." Their end, like ours, is one of such unspeakable glory or absolute horror, Lewis notes, that we could hardly bear either if we now experienced it.

No matter how mundane our experiences may seem to us, all of our work and play and passing on the street is really an encounter with immortal creatures who will one day either reflect back to us God's infinite beauty or unimaginable horror. From the man on the side of the street who you hardly notice to the woman standing in front of you in line at the post office, clicking her gum so loudly you can't help but notice her—each one is a potential future reflection of God's most unspeakable glory.

And our duty now, in this life, Lewis emphasizes, is to help others along toward their rightful end in God's presence. There is no greater weight or burden imaginable than this: the weight of glory.

FOR REFLECTION

1. Comparing our future glory in God's presence to fame seems like a dangerous idea. Why does C. S. Lewis insist that we must maintain this biblical image of glory? How would you express this to a nonbelieving friend?

2 When clarifying the idea of glory as luminosity as that of beholding unspeakable beauty, Lewis makes the curious claim that it is not enough to witness such beauty—that we want to be united with it. Can you think of some examples of this experience? How does this help explain the idea of our future glory as luminosity?

3 "When I read 'The Weight of Glory,'" Professor Tony Ash confesses, "it makes me want to go to heaven. ... There is nothing that Lewis has written that has this power on my life." Part of the lasting legacy of this sermon is its ability to help us see not only ourselves but our neighbors as bearers of God's infinite splendor, and that all of our interactions are thus of infinite importance. How will this reminder change the way you relate to your children? Your coworkers? Strangers?

WHY I LIKE
C. S. LEWIS

DID YOU KNOW?

In a 1962 issue of *The Christian Century*, C. S. Lewis was asked to name the top ten most influential books on his own life. His list included:

1. *Phantastes* by George MacDonald
2. *The Everlasting Man* by G. K. Chesterton
3. *The Aeneid* by Virgil
4. *The Temple* by George Herbert
5. *The Prelude* by William Wordsworth
6. *The Idea of the Holy* by Rudolf Otto
7. *The Consolation of Philosophy* by Boethius
8. *Life of Samuel Johnson* by James Boswell
9. *Descent into Hell* by Charles Williams
10. *Theism and Humanism* by Arthur James Balfour

C. S. Lewis had a nearly photographic memory, leading many to suggest that he was able to recite everything he had ever read.

WHY I LIKE C. S. LEWIS

Fᴿᴏᴍ C. S. Lᴇᴡɪs's ғᴏʀᴍᴇʀ ᴏғғɪᴄᴇ ᴀᴛ ᴛʜᴇ Kɪʟɴs, ᴡʜᴇʀᴇ ʜᴇ would have enjoyed a beautiful view of the garden and forest, Professor Tony Ash begins this final episode of our *Walking with C. S. Lewis* study. After the many books, sermons, and essays we've discussed, Professor Ash concludes this series with a personal reflection on why he appreciates C. S. Lewis and his work so much. We will turn now to these reflections.

VARIETY OF LITERARY GENRES

First, Professor Ash shares his appreciation for the sheer variety of literary genres that Lewis's literary works represent. Lewis's writings include:

- apologetics
- allegory
- fiction
- radio talks
- myth
- children's literature

- essays
- letters
- autobiography
- poetry
- science fiction
- word studies
- literary criticism

One of the most frequent questions I'm asked when teaching on C. S. Lewis is: "Who do you think is the modern-day equivalent to C. S. Lewis?" And one of the most unique features of Lewis's work that I point out in response to this question is the incredible variety of Lewis's writing. Even if we can think of someone whose apologetic work compares to Lewis's, it's highly unlikely that the same person has also published children's literature that has become a modern classic with global recognition, for example. The sheer number of genres in which Lewis has not only written but also left a unique legacy is quite remarkable.

REMARKABLE MEMORY

C. S. Lewis is widely recognized as one of the great intellectuals of the twentieth century, proven not only by his academic accomplishments (one of the few to earn a triple first from Oxford University), but also by his literary contributions on many different topics, from medieval literature to theology. But one often-overlooked feature of Lewis's intellect that Professor Ash shares his appreciation for is Lewis's remarkable memory. Lewis's uncanny ability to remember anything he had ever read has been recounted by his former students as well as his friends and family. But perhaps most impressive is the story of students picking a book at random from Lewis's library in his Magdalene College office and reading a line, to which Lewis would reply with the line immediately preceding and immediately following lines of text.

EXCELLENT APOLOGIST

As much as any other legacy C. S. Lewis left behind, Lewis is remembered today as one of the great apologists, or defenders, of the Christian faith. Professor Ash notes that this is one of the things that tops his list of favorite things about Lewis. In particular, Professor Ash shares that what he appreciates most about Lewis's approach to Christian apologetics, and where his apologetic work stands out most from the crowd, is his relentless pursuit of truth.

In his unapologetic pursuit of Christianity's ability to deal with the messy and complicated realities of our experiences in this world and the mystery of God, Lewis leaves no rock unturned. Not only does he ask the difficult questions we've thought of and wish we had the courage to ask—be it about suffering and miracles or about the reality of heaven and hell—but he asks those questions that are beyond our own imaginations. And even as he pursues the answers to those questions as far as he can go, he offers to us all the findings of his own wrestling with those questions in lucid explanations and illustrations that are equally logical and imaginative. Indeed, it is Lewis's refusal of easy answers that have made him such a revered apologist for the Christian faith.

NOT INTIMIDATED

Similarly, it is Lewis's own refusal to be intimidated by the intellectual opposition to Christianity that has given so many Christians following after him the courage to live into their own faith. Whether he could have seen the New Atheism and its heavy-handed intellectual critiques of Christianity—and all religion, for that matter—coming on the horizon or not, C. S. Lewis's work has shown that, when it comes to intellectual critiques, Christianity holds water. Studying and teaching at one of the world's premier intellectual communities, Lewis showed that it is not only possible to be a Christian intellectual, but that, for many, it is a calling which we have been called to live into.

WRITES FOR POPULAR CONSUMPTION

Of course, many intellectuals have come and gone, producing great amounts of work that the vast majority of the population will never be able to access. But one of the most distinguishing marks of C. S. Lewis's work, and another aspect of Lewis's writing that Professor Ash appreciates, is that his work is often written in such a way that others, regardless of whether they possess his intellectual gifts, can access and enjoy reading his thoughts. Lewis was gifted is in his ability to take top-shelf ideas and put them on the lower rungs for the rest of us—as he does, for example, when he shows how the fact that a square can exist as both an individual square and, simultaneously, an essential piece of a cube reveals something about the mystery of the three-in-one nature of the Trinity (see *Mere Christianity* for Lewis's full explanation).

Not only does Lewis make the lofty accessible, though; he does so in a richly satisfying way, thanks to his wonderful imagination. The genius of Lewis's highly popular *The Screwtape Letters*, for example, is not only its ability to pull back the veil on sin's evil, upside-down logic, but for doing so with such a vivid and relatable tone. Never lacking in wit or vibrant descriptions, Lewis's writing makes the complex equally delightful and clear.

QUOTABLE AND MEMORABLE

One of the other reasons for C. S. Lewis's lasting legacy is that his writing is so very quotable. Professor Ash admits from his own pastoral experience that his congregants would often notice when he *hadn't* quoted Lewis in a sermon! Many other Christian writers, pastors, and scholars have noted a similar reliance on Lewis in their thinking and teaching—pastor and author Timothy Keller, for example.

Some of Professor Ash's favorite C. S. Lewis quotes come from *Letters to Malcolm: Chiefly on Prayer*; *The Great Divorce*; *The Last Battle*; and *The Problem of Pain*.

HELPS DEFEND AGAINST TEMPTATION

One of Professor Ash's most personal reasons for appreciating Lewis's work is its ability to help defend against temptation. "No matter what we do otherwise, we've got to deal with being in a place where we are appealed to by God and where we're appealed to by the other power," Professor Ash points out. "Lewis has reminded me that ... every immorality is a moral breakdown."

We were made for God, Professor Ash goes on to note, which means that every time we allow temptation to move us away from God and toward sin, we are not only dishonoring our creator, but we are also doing great damage to our very being. So how does Lewis help us defend against the temptation to do evil? Lewis reminds us that, rather than viewing our desires as too strong when we are led to sinful behavior, we ought, instead, to see that they are not too strong, but simply askew. If we were, in fact, created for God, then all of our desires ultimately point us to God. Whenever we are tempted to evil, we are forgetting the ultimate end of our desires. By keeping our end in mind, we can guard against the temptation for our desires to be led astray from God.

SECTION TWO

TOWARD VIGOROUS REASONING, AWAY FROM SENTIMENTALITY

O NE OF THE THEMES THAT PROFESSOR ASH HAS OBSERVED throughout the works we've studied in this series is Lewis's insistence on reason, rather than following along with the contemporary fixation on emotions. Taking Lewis's conversion to Christianity as an example, Professor Ash insists that Lewis's return to the Christian faith did not come about because of a moving worship service or emotional appeal, but after a series of vigorous, thoughtful conversations and much reflection.

While it would be misguided to suggest that we are all wired with the exact same disposition or personality type with the same taste as Lewis for logic and reason-based appeals, Professor Ash is right to put his finger on what is, in many cases, an overemphasis on emotional appeals—whether in terms of how we discern potential spouses or in thinking about how we present the gospel. One of Lewis's great contributions is to reveal this over-reliance on our feelings. The good news of Jesus Christ, for example, is good news not because of the feelings it produces in us, but because it is true.

Likewise, for those in a committed marriage, emotions can be misleading, as Professor Ash notes, because emotions come and go. So long as we use our emotions to gauge how we relate to our spouse, we will fail to live up to our marital vows. But if our commitment to love our spouse is more important than our circumstances or feelings on any given day, then we are much more likely to enjoy the fruits of marriage God intends for us.

In our study of *The Screwtape Letters*, we discussed Lewis's idea of the "law of undulation," which reminds us that by nature of our physical and spiritual being, we will necessarily experience ebbs and flows in our life, regardless of our intimacy of God. Just because we're experiencing a difficult season, for example, does not mean that we're far from God—in fact, the very opposite may be true! What matters is not how we're feeling on a particularly day, but our intentional devotion to God.

Whether it is in terms of our relationships, our faith, or otherwise, C. S. Lewis has helped Professor Ash and many others by encouraging his readers to rely less on their emotions and more on thoughtful consideration of the facts of reality.

COMMITTED TO UNITY

I N A LARGELY FRACTURED CHRISTIANITY, WHERE BELIEVERS ARE more likely to identify with what makes them distinct from their brothers and sisters in Christ than to focus on what unites them, Professor Ash emphasizes his gratitude for C. S. Lewis's commitment to Christian unity. As Professor Ash points out, Lewis was himself a member of the Church of England, yet you never find him trying to convert anyone to his denomination. Instead, he encourages others to come to Christ—without a particular denominational specification.

Thinking back to our study of C. S. Lewis's book *Mere Christianity*, we are reminded of his analogy of the Christian household, which contains one central hallway, common to the entire house, as well as individual rooms, marked off from other rooms. The rooms in this analogy are like the different traditions or denominations within the same Christianity, each with their own distinguishing marks but all still proclaiming the same faith in our risen Lord. Lewis's goal was not to bring others to his particular room, but into the common faith.

Lewis was no stranger to a debate, but he refused to debate his friends on the inferiority or superiority of various Christian traditions. Whether the Lord's Supper should be understood this way or that was of little interest to Lewis, and certainly not worth debating, he suggested, precisely because it did not encourage unity. And unity is something our Lord takes very seriously (John 17:20–23). So, too, must we. "Be kind to those who have chosen different doors and to those who are still in the hall," Lewis writes. "If they are wrong they need your prayers all the more; and if they are your enemies, then you are under orders to pray for them" (preface, *Mere Christianity*).

Christians are to strive toward unity among their sisters and brothers rather than resorting to so much time spent trying to prove that their own particular tradition is superior to others. This is one of the great lessons that Professor Ash has taken from C. S. Lewis's work.

PERSONAL FAITH

One of the other great lessons Professor Ash has taken from Lewis's writing is that he is nearly always making a personal appeal to the reader. Though Lewis may not fit perfectly with our expectations of an evangelical Christian—depending, of course, on who you ask—his writing was perfectly evangelical in that he was concerned with inviting readers to live into the Christian tradition for themselves. At the end of so many chapters of *Mere Christianity*, for example, Lewis encourages readers that right here, right now, they have the opportunity to take seriously the claims of Christianity and to live them. As a result, Lewis's faith was contagious; the fire that had been fanned into a flame inside of him by God's grace and the faith of others produced light in so many other lives. May the same be true of each of our faith walks.

A CASE FOR ABSOLUTES

In a pluralistic, postmodern culture in which absolute values and morality are frequently traded for "what's right for you," C. S. Lewis's work stands out for his insistence in objective virtues. This, too, is an aspect of Lewis's work that Professor Ash highly values.

There are many places in Lewis's writing in which his insistence on absolutes can be found—such as *Mere Christianity* and *That Hideous Strength*. As Professor Ash notes, though it is one of Lewis's most dense works, *The Abolition of Man* makes an astounding case for absolute values that do not change, no matter the season or climate of our contemporary culture. Humans can no more argue against the idea of absolute, objective values, C. S. Lewis insists, than they can create an entirely new system of virtues. That is why any attempt to write off all of the virtues history has handed down as simply "old fashioned" is ultimately hopeless.

In our postmodern context, Lewis's insistence on the undeniable reality of absolute virtues is, for many, a refreshing perspective.

PERSON OF PRAYER

Concluding on a more personal note, Professor Ash admits his deep appreciation for C. S. Lewis's commitment to prayer. Far from writing off prayer as a childish practice that a man of his intellect does not need, Lewis frequently talks about his own prayer life, encourages others to do the same, and even asks those to whom he was writing to remember him in their prayers. Written at the very end of his career and published after his death, *Letters to Malcolm: Chiefly on Prayer* is a series of letters Lewis wrote to a fictional friend on the subject of prayer. In this book, readers can find Lewis's thoughts on a variety of different types of prayer, from communal and liturgical to private and petitionary prayer. This writing is not based in years of studying prayer in a clinical or academic setting, but out of his own experience as a devoted man of prayer. And one of the greatest lessons of prayer, for C. S. Lewis as much as for any one of us, is that it reminds us of our absolute need for and dependence on God, which is not a lesson we will ever advance beyond in this life.

FOR REFLECTION

1 Taking a moment to think back on our study of so many of C. S. Lewis's works, what has been your most favorite lesson from his writing? What will you take from this study?

2 After completing this study, what work(s) of Lewis's do you plan to pick up for the first time? What work(s) do you plan to reread? Why?

3 In what ways has this study of Lewis's work contributed to your own Christian growth? What is an area in your own faith in which this study has helped you realize your need for continued growth?

ABOUT THE AUTHOR

Ryan J. Pemberton has degrees in theology from Duke Divinity School and Oxford University, where he lived in C. S. Lewis's former home, served as president of the Oxford University C. S. Lewis Society, and cofounded the Oxford Open Forum, an interreligious dialogue group. Ryan has written for *Christianity Today*, *Image Journal*, Duke University chapel, *Bible Study Magazine*, *Relevant Magazine*, and *To An Unknown God*; his memoir, *Called: My Journey to C. S. Lewis's House and Back Again*, traces his time in Oxford. Ryan currently serves as minister for university engagement at First Presbyterian Church of Berkeley. He lives in the San Francisco Bay Area with his wife and their two children.

NOTES

EPISODE TWO: *THE SCREWTAPE LETTERS*

1. *The Collected Letters of C.S. Lewis* (San Francisco: HarperOne, 2004), 2:426.

2. Hans Urs von Balthasar, *Dare We Hope "That All Men Be Saved?": With a Short Discourse on Hell* (San Francisco: Ignatius Press, 1988), 187.

EPISODE FOUR: C. S. LEWIS'S LIFE

1. W. H. Lewis, ed., *The Lewis Papers*, 4:279.

2. C. S. Lewis, *They Stand Together: The Letters of C. S. Lewis to Arthur Greeves (1914-1963)* (New York: HarperCollins, 1979).

3. *The Collected Letters of C.S. Lewis* (San Francisco: HarperOne, 2004), 1:749.

4. Alister McGrath, *C. S. Lewis—A Life: Eccentric Genius, Reluctant Prophet* (Carol Stream, IL: Tyndale House Publishers, Inc., 2013), 282.

EPISODE SIX: NARNIA, PART I

1. *Collected Letters*, 3:848.

2. "Tools Inadequate and Incomplete: C.S. Lewis and the Great Religions," in *The Pilgrim's Guide: C.S. Lewis and the Art of Witness*, ed. David Mills (Grand Rapids, MI: Eerdmans, 1998), 231.

EPISODE NINE: *A GRIEF OBSERVED* AND "THE WEIGHT OF GLORY"

1. Buechner, *Secrets in the Dark*, 149.